BICENTENNIAL
MINUTES

BICENTENNIAL
MINUTES

Bicentennial Minutes
(New York's Role in the
Ratification of the Constitution)

A compilation of articles originally published
in the *New York State Bar News*

Edited by Daniel M. Kittay

Production Editor, Brad Carr

Designed by The Type & Design Center, Inc.
Latham, N.Y.

Published by the
Charles Evans Hughes Press

An affiliate of The New York Bar Foundation
One Elk Street, Albany, New York 12207

Cover Photo by Jon Jameson: Originally painted in 1938 by Gerald Foster, this mural illustrates the moment of compromise reached at the Dutchess County Courthouse on July 26, 1788, when delegates to the New York Ratification Convention approved the proposed United States Constitution. At left center, Governor George Clinton grasps the hand of Alexander Hamilton as Melancton Smith, John Jay, and Robert R. Livingston look on. With a vote of thirty to twenty-seven, New York became the eleventh state to ratify the United States Constitution and the eleventh pillar of the federal republic. This mural is permanently displayed in the United States Post Office, Poughkeepsie. Left to right: Philip Van Cortlandt, Cornelius Schoonmaker, Peter Vrooman, John Haring, Israel Thompson, Chancellor Robert R. Livingston, Melancton Smith, Governor George Clinton, Alexander Hamilton, Abraham Bancker, John Jay, James Clinton, Isaac Roosevelt, John Sloss Hobart, Jacobus Swartwout, Peter Vandervoort, James Duane, Philip Livingston, John Lansing, Lewis Morris, Richard Morris, Dirck Wyncoop, Gozen Ryerss.

Fortunately, a key to the figures in the mural was prepared by the staff of the Franklin D. Roosevelt Library in Hyde Park. George Clinton, encouraged by Melancton Smith, turns his back to the observer as Alexander Hamilton relishes the moment of victory; former New York State Chief Judge John Jay and Chancellor Robert R. Livingston, robed in black, add dignity to the scene. The solemn occasion is relieved by a curious witness — a mouse peeping from a hole in the woodwork.

Courtesy of U.S. Post Office, Poughkeepsie, N.Y., Mary J. Bordonaro, Postmaster.

Page 9 Alton S. Tobey's famous painting portraying the signing of the Constitution at Independence Hall in Philadelphia. The painting is titled, "The Signing of the Constitution, Philadelphia, September 17, 1787."

The photograph is courtesy of West Publishing Company, Copyright 1986.

Photographs: pages 18, 23, 25, 29, 30, 31, 35, 36, 37, 41, 42, 43, 47, 48, 49, 52, 58, 59, are from the The New-York Historical Society and its exhibition, "Government by Choice", Inventing the United States Constitution.

Page 19 The Atwater-Kent Museum, Philadelphia, Pa.

Page 24 Connecticut Historical Society, Hartford, Conn.

Page 53 David Sharpe, Alexandria, Va. taken for Project '87 (a joint project of the American Historical Association and the American Political Science Association), Washington, D.C. This poster is one of twelve which make up an exhibit on the Constitution entitled, *The Blessings of Liberty.* For more information on the exhibit, contact Project '87, 1527 New Hampshire Ave. N.W., Washington, D.C. 20036; (202) 483-2512.

Page 63 Culver Pictures, New York City, N.Y.
Published by the Charles Evans Hughes Press, Albany, N.Y., an affiliate of The New York Bar Foundation.

Library of Congress Catalog Card Number: 88-8802
ISBN 0-911129-09-X
Library of Congress Cataloging-in-Publication Data
Bicentennial Minutes.
   Originally published in State Bar news as a column under title: Bicentennial minute.
"The Constitution of the United States": p.
   1. United States—Constitutional history.
   2. New York (State)—Constitutional history.
      I. Kittay, Daniel M.
      II. United States. Constitution. 1988.
      III. State Bar news.
      KF4541.A2B53   1988   342.73'029   88-8802
      ISBN 0-911129-09-X   347.30229

Table of Contents

Introduction

by the Honorable Sol Wachtler, Chief Judge and Chairman of The New York State Commission on the Bicentennial of the U.S. Constitution

I often take pride in reflecting on the fact that it was here in New York State that the Congress of the Confederation called for a rewriting of the Articles of Confederation to be held in Philadelphia. You see, the Miracle at Philadelphia began in New York. But not long after their arrival in Philadelphia it became clear the Framers were there to do something more than the splinting and patching of a collapsing set of Articles — they were there to build a nation.

We are now celebrating the 200th anniversary of that Constitution—of the birth of our nation — and by any standard of which I am aware, our celebration will be justified.

The celebration of our Constitution will not be marked by fireworks and tall ships. It will be a celebration of reflection.

When we celebrated the 100th birthday of the Statue of Liberty, we were reminded that we are the children of a nation of immigrants. Some of those immigrants were our own parents, or grandparents. Many spoke an alien language, most were poor and uneducated. Some came to these shores as slaves. Perhaps most significantly, they lacked both knowledge and experience with the democratic process. That they survived — and in fact thrived — is a testament not only to their own fortitude, but to the foresight of our constitutional forebears, and to the seeds of a just government which they planted so firmly. We can be rightly proud of our Constitution, for those who came before us did their work well.

Yet we would be negligent to be satisfied with a mere celebration of the past. Celebrations are also a time for examination — to consider where we are now, what the future holds in store for us, and whether that future will see the survival of this great constitutional experiment.

Examination begins with understanding. We are indebted to The New York Bar Foundation and the New York State Bar Association, as well as the Charles Evans Hughes Press, publisher of this magnificent book for presenting the articles and pictures which allow us the opportunity to reflect and to examine — an opportunity which brings us closer to that understanding.

Foreword

by Maryann Saccomando Freedman
President, New York State Bar Association

Being President of this Association in this Bicentennial year has been an incomparable experience; so many thrilling projects and special events; such exciting opportunities to reinforce our cherished heritage and the challenge it represents. It is indeed an honor and a privilege to be a part of the production of these "Bicentennial Minutes."

While it seems amazing today to think that there was any question of accepting our Constitution, the truth is that in the post-Revolution raw politics of 1788, the people of the nation were deeply divided on the issue of ratification. Nowhere were the issues drawn more clearly or dramatically than in New York State as the lines were drawn between agrarian and commercial interests, rural and urban interests, states righters and those who favored a strong, central government. Passions ran high among New York's 50,000 inhabitants and the debate whether to ratify was one of the most lively and spirited in our history, replete with wit, invective, grand speeches, dirty tricks, parades, demonstrations, and even public brawls. All of this is captured vividly in these Bicentennial Minutes.

Happily, the debate culminated in New York's ratification at Poughkeepsie on July 26, 1788. As one of the most populous and commercially powerful states at that time, New York's ratification was vital to the success of any Union.

The delegates who had earlier assembled in convention in Philadelphia were not perfect men. Divided by regional loyalties, possessed of tremendous egos, vulnerable to the pressures of politics and susceptible to human frailties, they, nevertheless, had a vision of a strong and just nation, a government that would establish justice, bring order to chaos, ensure domestic tranquility, provide for the defense, promote the welfare, and secure blessings of liberty to its people.

Built upon compromise, the system of separation of powers and the checks and balances they devised among a bicameral Legislature, a Judiciary and an Executive Branch has given us a stable government subject to the will of "We the people." The acknowledged "unalienable rights" possessed by "We the people," subsequently guaranteed by the Bill of Rights, has made us a free people.

But, "We the people" still have much to do. The dream set down on that piece of parchment preserved under glass must be made a reality for every American. Its promise must be secured for future generations. As the actor portraying Alexander Hamilton explains in his monologue in the movie, "An Empire of Reason," "This government is not only a government for us, but for our children's children — for times and situations that none of us can imagine..."

The Bicentennial challenges us to renew and redouble our efforts to serve the law and to be worthy of being called lawyers. This our Association pledges to do.

On behalf of the New York State Bar Association, I express my sincere appreciation to Nicole A. Gordon and the members of the Committee on Federal Constitution for giving us this splendid reference work.

Message

by Nicole A. Gordon
Chair, Committee on Federal Constitution
of the New York State Bar Association

Some years ago, the Committee on Federal Constitution began to contemplate what its contribution to the celebration on the Bicentennial of the Constitution should be. A particular and unique approach emerged: the committee would put its efforts into projects that filled a gap between, on the one hand, the worthy scholarly projects that would find their audience primarily among the sophisticated Bar and, on the other, the celebratory occasions that would fill the need for festive public displays of the excitement of the moment. Between these two extremes the committee decided to sponsor projects that would help to educate a wide audience, preferably in a manner that would be attractive, not just to members of the Bar, but also to those not accustomed to thinking about — much less grappling with — constitutional issues.

The focus, naturally, would be New York's pivotal role in the constitutional debates of the period.

We believed that we, as lawyers, might claim a special authority to speak on matters relating to the Constitution; we also believed that as lawyers we had a special responsibility to the public to be part of an effort to elevate the level of discussion above the parades and at the same time make it understandable to non-lawyers.

With this goal in mind, the committee engaged in projects intended for the broadest possible audience. For one of these projects, members of the committee composed the "Bicentennial Minutes" appearing in this book, under the able direction of Sheldon Siporin, a member of the Committee on Federal Constitution, to whom we are indebted. The Minutes were initially prepared for publication in the *State Bar News,* but always with the hope and expectation that they would be compiled for wider distribution. This book realizes the committee's aim. It was conceived and executed by Brad Carr, Director of Communications and Public Affairs for the Association, to whom many thanks are also due.

When George Washington was sworn in — in New York City — as the first President of the United States, he referred to the new Constitutional government as an "experiment entrusted to the hands of the American people." That experiment can continue to endure only if we continue to study it with care and heed the lessons of its history. As members of the Bar, therefore, we can do no greater good as part of our Bicentennial celebration than to convey the interest and complexity of the issues that faced the Framers and continue to confront us today.

I hope you, the readers of these Minutes, will find them entertaining, colorful, engaging, thoughtful, and above all, informative and educational. If you share them with your colleagues, friends, and family, they will especially have served their purpose.

Alton S. Tobey's famous painting portraying the signing of the Constitution at Independence Hall in Phil-adelphia. The painting is titled, "The Signing of the Constitution, Philadelphia, September 17, 1787."

The Constitution of the United States

We the People of the United States, in Order to form a more perfect Union, establish Justice, insure domestic Tranquility, provide for the common defence, promote the general Welfare, and secure the Blessings of Liberty to ourselves and our Posterity, do ordain and establish this Constitution for the United States of America.

Article. I.

Section. 1. All legislative Powers herein granted shall be vested in a Congress of the United States, which shall consist of a Senate and House of Representatives.

Section. 2. The House of Representatives shall be composed of Members chosen every second Year by the People of the several States, and the Electors in each State shall have the Qualifications requisite for Electors of the most numerous Branch of the State Legislature.

No Person shall be a Representative who shall not have attained to the Age of twenty five Years, and been seven Years a Citizen of the United States, and who shall not, when elected, be an Inhabitant of that State in which he shall be chosen.

[Representatives and direct Taxes shall be apportioned among the several States which may be included within this Union, according to their respective Numbers, which shall be determined by adding to the whole Number of free Persons, including those bound to Service for a Term of Years, and excluding Indians not taxed, three fifths of all other Persons.]* The actual Enumeration shall be made within three Years after the first Meeting of the Congress of the United States, and within every subsequent Term of ten Years, in such Manner as they shall by Law direct. The number of Representatives shall not exceed one for every thirty Thousand, but each State shall have at Least one Representative; and until such enumeration shall be made, the State of New Hampshire shall be entitled to chuse three, Massachusetts eight, Rhode-Island and Providence Plantations one, Connecticut five, New-York six, New Jersey four, Pennsylvania eight, Delaware one, Maryland six, Virginia ten, North Carolina five, South Carolina five, and Georgia three.

When vacancies happen in the Representation from any State, the Executive Authority thereof shall issue Writs of Election to fill such Vacancies.

The House of Representatives shall chuse their Speaker and other Officers; and shall have the sole Power of Impeachment.

Section. 3. The Senate of the United States shall be composed of two Senators from each State, [chosen by the Legisla-

*Changed by section 2 of the Fourteenth Amendment.

ture thereof,]* for six Years; and each Senator shall have one Vote.

Immediately after they shall be assembled in Consequence of the first Election, they shall be divided as equally as may be into three Classes. The Seats of the Senators of the first Class shall be vacated at the Expiration of the second Year, of the second Class at the Expiration of the fourth Year, and of the third Class at the Expiration of the sixth Year, so that one third may be chosen every second Year; [and if Vacancies happen by Resignation, or otherwise, during the Recess of the Legislature of any State, the Executive thereof may make temporary Appointments until the next Meeting of the Legislature, which shall then fill such Vacancies.]*

No Person shall be a Senator who shall not have attained to the Age of thirty Years, and been nine Years a Citizen of the United States, and who shall not, when elected, be an Inhabitant of that State for which he shall be chosen.

The Vice President of the United States shall be President of the Senate, but shall have no Vote, unless they be equally divided.

The Senate shall chuse their other Officers and also a President pro tempore, in the Absence of the Vice President, or when he shall exercise the Office of President of the United States.

The Senate shall have the sole Power to try all Impeachments. When sitting for that Purpose, they shall be on Oath or Affirmation. When the President of the United States is tried, the Chief Justice shall preside: And no Person shall be convicted without the Concurrence of two thirds of the Members present.

Judgment in Cases of Impeachment shall not extend further than to removal from Office, and disqualification to hold and enjoy any Office of honor, Trust or Profit under the United States: but the Party convicted shall nevertheless be liable and subject to Indictment, Trial, Judgment and Punishment, according to Law.

Section. 4. The Times, Places and Manner of holding Elections for Senators and Representatives shall be prescribed in each State by the Legislature thereof; but the Congress may at any time by Law make or alter such Regulations, except as to the Places of chusing Senators.

The Congress shall assemble at least once in every Year, and such Meeting shall be [on the first Monday in December,]** unless they shall by Law appoint a different Day.

Section. 5. Each House shall be the Judge of the Elections, Returns and Qualifications of its own Members, and a Majority of each shall constitute a Quorum to do Business; but a smaller Number may adjourn from day to day, and may be authorized to compel the Attendance of absent Members, in such Manner, and under such Penalties as each House may provide.

Each House may determine the Rules of its Proceedings, punish its Members for disorderly Behaviour, and, with the Concurrence of two thirds, expel a Member.

Each House shall keep a Journal of its Proceedings, and from time to time publish the same, excepting such Parts as may in their Judgment require Secrecy; and the Yeas and Nays of the Members of either House on any question shall, at the Desire of one fifth of those Present, be entered on the Journal.

Neither House during the Session of Congress, shall, without the Consent of the other, adjourn for more than three days, nor

*Changed by the Seventeenth Amendment.

**Changed by section 2 of the Twentieth Amendment.

to any other Place than that in which the two Houses shall be sitting.

Section. 6. The Senators and Representatives shall receive a Compensation for their Services, to be ascertained by Law, and paid out of the Treasury of the United States. They shall in all Cases except Treason, Felony and Breach of the Peace, be privileged from Arrest during their Attendance at the Session of their respective Houses, and in going to and returning from the same; and for any Speech or Debate in either House, they shall not be questioned in any other Place.

No Senator or Representative shall, during the Time for which he was elected, be appointed to any civil Office under the Authority of the United States, which shall have been created, or the Emoluments whereof shall have been encreased during such time; and no Person holding any Office under the United States, shall be a Member of either House during his Continuance in Office.

Section. 7. All Bills for raising Revenue shall originate in the House of Representatives; but the Senate may propose or concur with Amendments as on other Bills.

Every Bill which shall have passed the House of Representatives and the Senate, shall, before it becomes a Law, be presented to the President of the United States; If he approve he shall sign it, but if not he shall return it, with his Objections to that House in which it shall have originated, who shall enter the Objections at large on their Journal, and proceed to reconsider it. If after such Reconsideration two thirds of that House shall agree to pass the Bill, it shall be sent, together with the Objections, to the other House, by which it shall likewise be reconsidered, and if approved by two thirds of that House, it shall become a Law. But in all such Cases the Votes of both Houses shall be determined by yeas and Nays, and the Names of the Persons voting for and against the Bill shall be entered on the Journal of each House respectively. If any Bill shall not be returned by the President within ten Days (Sundays excepted) after it shall have been presented to him, the Same shall be a Law, in like Manner as if he had signed it, unless the Congress by their Adjournment prevent its Return, in which Case it shall not be a Law.

Every Order, Resolution, or Vote to which the Concurrence of the Senate and House of Representatives may be necessary (except on a question of Adjournment) shall be presented to the President of the United States; and before the Same shall take Effect, shall be approved by him, or being disapproved by him, shall be repassed by two thirds of the Senate and House of Representatives, according to the Rules and Limitations prescribed in the Case of a Bill.

Section. 8. The Congress shall have Power To lay and collect Taxes, Duties, Imposts and Excises, to pay the Debts and provide for the common Defence and general Welfare of the United States; but all Duties, Imposts and Excises shall be uniform throughout the United States;

To borrow Money on the credit of the United States;

To regulate Commerce with foreign Nations, and among the several States, and with the Indian Tribes;

To establish an uniform Rule of Naturalization, and uniform Laws on the subject of Bankruptcies throughout the United States;

To coin Money, regulate the Value thereof, and of foreign Coin,

and fix the Standard of Weights and Measures;

To provide for the Punishment of counterfeiting the Securities and current Coin of the United States;

To establish Post Offices and post Roads;

To promote the Progress of Science and useful Arts, by securing for limited Times to Authors and Inventors the exclusive Right to their respective Writings and Discoveries;

To constitute Tribunals inferior to the supreme Court;

To define and punish Piracies and Felonies committed on the high Seas, and Offenses against the Law of Nations;

To declare War, grant Letters of Marque and Reprisal, and make Rules concerning Captures on Land and Water;

To raise and support Armies, but no Appropriation of Money to that Use shall be for a longer Term than two Years;

To provide and maintain a Navy;

To make Rules for the Government and Regulation of the land and naval Forces;

To provide for calling forth the Militia to execute the Laws of the Union, suppress Insurrections and repel Invasions;

To provide for organizing, arming, and disciplining, the Militia, and for governing such Part of them as may be employed in the Service of the United States, reserving to the States respectively, the Appointment of the Officers, and the Authority of training the Militia according to the discipline prescribed by Congress;

To exercise exclusive Legislation in all Cases whatsoever, over such District (not exceeding ten Miles square) as may, by Cession of particular States, and the Acceptance of Congress, become the Seat of the Government of the United States, and to exercise like Authority over all Places purchased by the Consent of the Legislature of the State in which the Same shall be, for the Erection of Forts, Magazines, Arsenals, dock-Yards and other needful Buildings; — And

To make all Laws which shall be necessary and proper for carrying into Execution the foregoing Powers, and all other Powers vested by this Constitution in the Government of the United States, or in any Department or Officer thereof.

Section. 9. The Migration or Importation of such Persons as any of the States now existing shall think proper to admit, shall not be prohibited by the Congress prior to the Year one thousand eight hundred and eight, but a Tax or duty may be imposed on such Importation, not exceeding ten dollars for each Person.

The Privilege of the Writ of Habeas Corpus shall not be suspended, unless when in Cases of Rebellion or Invasion the public Safety may require it.

No Bill of Attainder or ex post facto Law shall be passed.

[No Capitation, or other direct, Tax shall be laid, unless in Proportion to the Census or Enumeration herein before directed to be taken.]*

No Tax or Duty shall be laid on Articles exported from any State.

No Preference shall be given by any Regulation of Commerce or Revenue to the Ports of one State over those of another: nor shall Vessels bound to, or from, one State, be obliged to enter, clear, or pay Duties in another.

No Money shall be drawn from the Treasury, but in Consequence of Appropriations made by Law; and a regular State-

*Changed by the Sixteenth Amendment.

ment and Account of the Receipts and Expenditures of all public Money shall be published from time to time.

No Title of Nobility shall be granted by the United States: And no Person holding any Office of Profit or Trust under them, shall, without the Consent of the Congress, accept of any present, Emolument, Office, or Title, of any kind whatever, from any King, Prince, or foreign State.

Section. 10. No State shall enter into any Treaty, Alliance, or Confederation; grant Letters of Marque and Reprisal; coin Money; emit Bills of Credit; make any Thing but gold and silver Coin a Tender in Payment of Debts; pass any Bill of Attainder, ex post facto Law, or Law impairing the Obligation of Contracts, or grant any Title of Nobility.

No State shall, without the Consent of the Congress, lay any Imposts or Duties on Imports or Exports, except what may be absolutely necessary for executing it's inspection Laws: and the net Produce of all Duties and Imposts, laid by any State on Imports of Exports, shall be for the Use of the Treasury of the United States; and all such Laws shall be subject to the Revision and Controul of the Congress.

No State shall, without the Consent of Congress, lay any Duty of Tonnage, keep Troops, or Ships of War in time of Peace, enter into any Agreement or Compact with another State, or with a foreign Power, or engage in War, unless actually invaded, or in such imminent Danger as will not admit of delay.

Article. II.

Section. 1. The executive Power shall be vested in a President of the United States of America. He shall hold his Office during the Term of four Years, and, together with the Vice President, chosen for the same Term, be elected, as follows

Each State shall appoint, in such Manner as the Legislature thereof may direct, a Number of Electors, equal to the whole Number of Senators and Representatives to which the State may be entitled in the Congress: but no Senator or Representative, or Person holding an Office of Trust or Profit under the United States, shall be appointed an Elector.

[The Electors shall meet in their respective States, and vote by Ballot for two Persons, of whom one at least shall not be an Inhabitant of the same State with themselves. And they shall make a List of all the Persons voted for, and of the Number of Votes for each; which List they shall sign and certify, and transmit sealed to the Seat of the Government of the United States, directed to the President of the Senate. The President of the Senate shall, in the Presence of the Senate and House of Representatives, open all the Certificates, and the Votes shall then be counted. The Person having the greatest Number of Votes shall be the President, if such Number be a Majority of the whole Number of Electors appointed; and if there be more than one who have such Majority, and have an equal Number of Votes, then the House of Representatives shall immediately chuse by Ballot one of them for President; and if no Person have a Majority, then from the five highest on the List the said House shall in like Manner chuse the President. But in chusing the President, the Votes shall be taken by States, the Representation from each State having one Vote; A quorum for this Purpose shall consist of a Member or Members from two thirds of the States, and a Majority of all the States shall be necessary to a Choice. In every Case, after the Choice of the President, the Person having the greatest Number of Votes of the Electors shall be the Vice President. But if there should remain two or more who have equal Votes, the Senate shall chuse from them by Ballot the Vice President.]*

The Congress may determine the Time of chusing the Electors, and the Day on which they shall give their Votes; which Day shall be the same throughout the United States.

No Person except a natural born Citizen, or a Citizen of the United States, at the time of the Adoption of this Constitution, shall be eligible to the Office of the President; neither shall any person be eligible to that Office who shall not have attained to the Age of thirty five Years, and been fourteen Years a Resident within the United States.

[In Case of the Removal of the President from Office, or of his Death, Resignation, or Inability to discharge the Powers and Duties of the said Office, the Same shall devolve on the Vice President, and the Congress may by Law provide for the Case of Removal, Death, Resignation or Inability, both of the President and Vice President, declaring what Officer shall then act as President, and such Officer shall act accordingly, until the Disability be removed, or a President shall be elected.]**

The President shall, at stated Times, receive for his Services, a Compensation, which shall neither be increased nor diminished during the Period for which he shall have been elected, and he shall not receive within that Period any other Emolument from the United States, or any of them.

Before he enter on the Execution of his Office, he shall take the following Oath or Affirmation:—"I do solemnly swear (or affirm) that I will faithfully execute the Office of President of the United States, and will to the best of my Ability, preserve, protect and defend the Constitution of the United States."

Section. 2. The President shall be Commander in Chief of the Army and Navy of the United States, and of the Militia of the several States, when called into the actual Service of the United States; he may require the Opinion, in writing, of the principal Officer in each of the executive Departments, upon any Subject relating to the Duties of their respective Offices, and he shall have Power to grant Reprieves and Pardons for Offenses against the United States, except in Cases of Impeachment.

He shall have Power, by and with the Advice and Consent of the Senate, to make Treaties, provided two thirds of the Senators present concur; and he shall nominate, and by and with the Advice and Consent of the Senate, shall appoint Ambassadors, other public Ministers and Consuls, Judges of the supreme Court, and all other Officers of the United States, whose Appointments are not herein otherwise provided for, and which shall be established by Law: but the Congress may by Law vest the Appointment of such inferior Officers, as they think proper, in the President alone, in the Courts of Law, or in the Heads of Departments.

The President shall have Power to fill up all Vacancies that may happen during the Recess of the Senate, by granting Commissions which shall expire at the End of their next Session.

*Changed by the Twelfth Amendment.
**Changed by the Twenty-Fifth Amendment.

Section. 3. He shall from time to time give to the Congress Information of the State of the Union, and recommend to their Consideration such Measures as he shall judge necessary and expedient; he may, on extraordinary Occasions, convene both Houses, or either of them, and in Case of Disagreement between them, with Respect to the Time of Adjournment, he may adjourn them to such Time as he shall think proper; he shall receive Ambassadors and other public Ministers; he shall take Care that the Laws be faithfully executed, and shall Commission all the Officers of the United States.

Section. 4. The President, Vice President and all civil Officers of the United States, shall be removed from Office on Impeachment for, and Conviction of, Treason, Bribery, or other high Crimes and Misdemeanors.

Article. III.

Section. 1. The judicial Power of the United States, shall be vested in one supreme Court, and in such inferior Courts as the Congress may from time to time ordain and establish. The Judges, both of the supreme and inferior Courts, shall hold their Offices during good Behaviour, and shall, at stated Times, receive for their Services, a Compensation, which shall not be diminished during their Continuance in Office.

Section. 2. The judicial Power shall extend to all Cases, in Law and Equity, arising under this Constitution, the Laws of the United States, and Treaties made, or which shall be made, under their Authority;—to all Cases affecting Ambassadors, other public Ministers and Consuls;—to all Cases of admiralty and maritime Jurisdiction;—to Controversies to which the United States shall be a Party;—to Controversies between two or more States; [between a State and Citizens of another State;—]* between Citizens of different States—between Citizens of the same State claiming Lands under Grants of different States, [and between a State, or the Citizens thereof, and foreign States Citizens or Subjects.]*

In all Cases affecting Ambassadors, other public Ministers and Consuls, and those in which a State shall be Party, the supreme Court shall have original Jurisdiction. In all the other Cases before mentioned, the supreme Court shall have appellate Jurisdiction, both as to Law and Fact, with such Exceptions, and under such Regulations as the Congress shall make.

The Trial of all Crimes, except in Cases of Impeachment; shall be by Jury; and such Trial shall be held in the State where the said Crimes shall have been committed; but when not committed within any State, the Trial shall be at such Place or Places as the Congress may by Law have directed.

Section. 3. Treason against the United States, shall consist only in levying War against them, or in adhering to their Enemies, giving them Aid and Comfort. No Person shall be convicted of Treason unless on the Testimony of two Witnesses to the same overt Act, or on Confession in open Court.

The Congress shall have Power to declare the Punishment of Treason, but no Attainder of Treason shall work Corruption of Blood, or Forfeiture except during the Life of the Person attainted.

*Changed by the Eleventh Amendment.

Article. IV.

Section. 1. Full Faith and Credit shall be given in each State to the public Acts, Records, and judicial Proceedings of every other State; And the Congress may by general Laws prescribe the Manner in which such Acts, Records and Proceedings shall be proved, and the Effect thereof.

Section. 2. The Citizens of each State shall be entitled to all Privileges and Immunities of Citizens in the several States.

A Person charged in any State with Treason, Felony or other Crime, who shall flee from Justice, and be found in another State, shall on Demand of the executive Authority of the State from which he fled, be delivered up, to be removed to the State having Jurisdiction of the Crime.

[No Person held to Service or Labour in one State, under the Laws thereof, escaping into another, shall, in Consequence of any Law or Regulation therein, be discharged from such Service or Labour, but shall be delivered up on Claim of the Party to whom such Service or Labour may be due.]*

Section. 3. New States may be admitted by the Congress into this Union; but no new State shall be formed or erected within the Jurisdiction of any other State; nor any State be formed by the Junction of two or more States, or Parts of States without the Consent of the Legislatures of the States concerned as well as of the Congress.

The Congress shall have Power to dispose of and make all needful Rules and Regulations respecting the Territory or other Property belonging to the United States; and nothing in this Constitution shall be so construed as to Prejudice any Claims of the United States, or of any particular State.

Section. 4. The United States shall guarantee to every State in this Union a Republican Form of Government, and shall protect each of them against Invasion; and on Application of the Legislature, or of the Executive (when the Legislature cannot be convened) against domestic Violence.

Article. V.

The Congress, whenever two thirds of both Houses shall deem it necessary, shall propose Amendments to this Constitution, or, on the Application of the Legislatures of two thirds of the several States, shall call a Convention for proposing Amendments, which, in either Case, shall be valid to all Intents and Purposes, as Part of this Constitution, when ratified by the Legislatures of three fourths of the several States, or by Conventions in three fourths thereof, as the one or the other Mode of Ratification may be proposed by the Congress; Provided that no Amendment which may be made prior to the Year One thousand eight hundred and eight shall in any Manner affect the first and fourth Clauses in the Ninth Section of the first Article; and that no State, without its Consent, shall be deprived of it's equal Suffrage in the Senate.

Article. VI.

All Debts contracted and Engagements entered into, before the Adoption of this Constitution, shall be as valid against the United States under this Constitution, as under the Confederation.

*Changed by the Thirteenth Amendment.

This Constitution, and the Laws of the United States which shall be made in Pursuance thereof; and all Treaties made, or which shall be made, under the Authority of the United States, shall be the supreme Law of the Land; and the Judges in every State shall be bound thereby, any Thing in the Constitution or Laws of any State to the Contrary notwithstanding,

The Senators and Representatives before mentioned, and the Members of the several State Legislatures, and all executive and judicial Officers both of the United States and of the several States, shall be bound by Oath or Affirmation, to support this Constitution; but no religious Test shall ever be required as a Qualification to any Office or public Trust under the United States.

Article. VII.

The Ratification of the Conventions of nine States, shall be sufficient for the Establishment of this Constitution between the States so ratifying the Same.

done in Convention by the Unanimous Consent of the States present the Seventeenth Day of September in the Year of our Lord one thousand seven hundred and Eighty seven and of the Independence of the United States of America the Twelfth In Witness whereof We have hereunto subscribed our Names,

Go. Washington—Presidt.
and deputy from Virginia

New Hampshire John Langdon
Nicholas Gilman

Massachusetts Nathaniel Gorham
Rufus King

Connecticut Wm. Saml. Johnson
Roger Sherman

New York Alexander Hamilton

New Jersey Wil: Livingston
David Brearley
Wm. Paterson
Jona: Dayton

Pennsylvania B Franklin
Thomas Mifflin
Robt Morris
Geo. Clymer
Thos. FitzSimons
Jared Ingersoll
James Wilson
Gouv Morris

Delaware Geo: Read
Gunning Bedford jun
John Dickinson
Richard Bassett
Jaco: Broom

Maryland James McHenry
Dan of St Thos. Jenifer
Danl Carroll

Virginia John Blair—
James Madison Jr.

North Carolina Wm. Blount
Richd. Dobbs Spaight
Hu Williamson

South Carolina J. Rutledge
Charles Cotesworth Pinckney
Charles Pinckney
Pierce Butler

Georgia William Few
Abr Baldwin

Attest William Jackson Secretary

In Convention Monday September 17th 1787.

Present
The States of

New Hampshire, Massachusetts, Connecticut, Mr. Hamilton from New York, New Jersey, Pennsylvania, Delaware, Maryland, Virginia, North Carolina, South Carolina and Georgia.

Resolved

That the preceeding Constitution be laid before the United States in Congress assembled, and that it is the Opinion of this Convention, that it should afterwards be submitted to a Convention of Delegates, chosen in each State by the People thereof, under the Recommendation of its Legislature, for their Assent and Ratification; and that each Convention assenting to, and ratifying the Same, should give Notice thereof to the United States in Congress assembled. Resolved, That it is the Opinion of this Convention, that as soon as the Conventions of nine States shall have ratified this Constitution, the United States in Congress assembled should fix a Day on which Electors should be appointed by the States which shall have ratified the same, and a Day on which the Electors should assemble to vote for the President, and the Time and Place for commencing Proceedings under this Constitution.

That after such Publication the Electors should be appointed, and the Senators and Representatives elected: That the Electors should meet on the Day fixed for the Election of the President, and should transmit their Votes certified, signed, sealed and directed, as the Constitution requires, to the Secretary of the United States in Congress assembled, that the Senators and Representatives should convene at the Time and Place assigned; that the Senators should appoint a President of the Senate, for the sole Purpose of receiving, opening and counting the Votes for President; and, that after he shall be chosen, the Congress, together with the President, should, without Delay, proceed to execute this Constitution.

By the unanimous Order of the Convention

Go. WASHINGTON—Presidt.

W. JACKSON Secretary.

AMENDMENTS TO THE CONSTITUTION OF THE UNITED STATES OF AMERICA

ARTICLES IN ADDITION TO, AND AMENDMENT OF, THE CONSTITUTION OF THE UNITED STATES OF AMERICA, PROPOSED BY CONGRESS, AND RATIFIED BY THE SEVERAL STATES, PURSUANT TO THE FIFTH ARTICLE OF THE ORIGINAL CONSTITUTION.

Amendment I.*

Congress shall make no law respecting an establishment of religion, or prohibiting the free exercise thereof; or abridging the freedom of speech, or of the press, or the right of the people peaceably to assemble, and to petition the Government for a redress of grievances.

Amendment II.

A well regulated Militia, being necessary to the security of a free State, the right of the people to keep and bear Arms, shall not be infringed.

Amendment III.

No Soldier shall, in time of peace be quartered in any house, without the consent of the Owner, nor in time of war, but in a manner to be prescribed by law.

Amendment IV.

The right of the people to be secure in their persons, houses, papers, and effects, against unreasonable searches and seizures, shall not be violated, and no Warrants shall issue, but upon probable cause, supported by Oath or affirmation, and particularly describing the place to be searched, and the persons or things to be seized.

Amendment V.

No person shall be held to answer for a capital, or otherwise infamous crime, unless on a presentment or indictment of a Grand Jury, except in cases arising in the land or naval forces, or in the Militia, when in actual service in time of War or public danger; nor shall any person be subject for the same offence to be twice put in jeopardy of life or limb, nor shall be compelled in any criminal case to be a witness against himself, nor be deprived of life, liberty, or property, without due process of law; nor shall private property be taken for public use without just compensation.

*The first ten Amendments (Bill of Rights) were ratified effective December 15, 1791.

Amendment VI.

In all criminal prosecutions, the accused shall enjoy the right to a speedy and public trial, by an impartial jury of the State and district wherein the crime shall have been committed; which district shall have been previously ascertained by law, and to be informed of the nature and cause of the accusation; to be confronted with the witnesses against him; to have compulsory process for obtaining witnesses in his favor, and to have the assistance of counsel for his defence.

Amendment VII.

In Suits at common law, where the value in controversy shall exceed twenty dollars, the right of trial by jury shall be preserved, and no fact tried by a jury shall be otherwise re-examined in any Court of the United States, than according to the rules of the common law.

Amendment VIII.

Excessive bail shall not be required, nor excessive fines imposed, nor cruel and unusual punishments inflicted.

Amendment IX.

The enumeration in the Constitution of certain rights shall not be construed to deny or disparage others retained by the people.

Amendment X.

The powers not delegated to the United States by the Constitution, nor prohibited by it to the States, are reserved to the States respectively, or to the people.

Amendment XI.*

The Judicial power of the United States shall not be construed to extend to any suit in law or equity, commenced or prosecuted against one of the United States by Citizens of another State, or by Citizens or Subjects of any Foreign State.

Amendment XII.**

The Electors shall meet in their respective states, and vote by ballot for President and Vice President, one of whom, at least, shall not be an inhabitant of the same state with themselves; they shall name in their ballots the person voted for as President, and in distinct ballots the person voted for as Vice-President, and they shall make distinct lists of all persons voted for as President, and of all persons voted for as Vice-President, and of the number of votes for each, which lists they shall sign and certify, and transmit sealed to the seat of the government of the United States, directed to the President of the Senate;—The President of the Senate shall, in the presence of the Senate and House of Representatives, open all the certificates and the votes shall then be counted;—The person having the greatest number of votes for President shall be the President, if such number be a majority of the whole number of Electors appointed; and if no person have such majority, then from the persons having the highest numbers not exceeding three on the list of those voted for as Presi-

dent, the House of Representatives shall choose immediately, by ballot, the President. But in choosing the President, the votes shall be taken by states, the representation from each state having one vote; a quorum for this purpose shall consist of a member or members from two-thirds of the states, and a majority of all the states shall be necessary to a choice. [And if the House of Representatives shall not choose a President whenever the right of choice shall devolve upon them, before the fourth day of March next following, then the Vice-President shall act as President, as in the case of the death or other constitutional disability of the President—]* The person having the greatest number of votes as Vice-President, shall be the Vice-President, if such number be a majority of the whole number of Electors appointed, and if no person have a majority, then from the two highest numbers on the list, the Senate shall choose the Vice-President; a quorum for the purpose shall consist of two-thirds of the whole number of Senators, and a majority of the whole number shall be necessary to a choice. But no person constitutionally ineligible to the office of President shall be eligible to that of Vice-President of the United States.

Amendment XIII.**

Section 1. Neither slavery nor involuntary servitude, except as a punishment for crime whereof the party shall have been duly convicted, shall exist within the United States, or any place subject to their jurisdiction.

Section 2. Congress shall have power to enforce this article by appropriate legislation.

Amendment XIV.***

Section 1. All persons born or naturalized in the United States and subject to the jurisdiction thereof, are citizens of the United States and of the State wherein they reside. No State shall make or enforce any law which shall abridge the privileges or immunities of citizens of the United States; nor shall any State deprive any person of life, liberty, or property, without due process of law; nor deny to any person within its jurisdiction the equal protection of the laws.

Section 2. Representatives shall be apportioned among the several States according to their respective numbers, counting the whole number of persons in each State, excluding Indians not taxed. But when the right to vote at any election for the choice of electors for President and Vice President of the United States, Representatives in Congress, the Executive and Judicial officers of a State, or the members of the Legislature thereof, is denied to any of the male inhabitants of such State, being twenty-one years of age, and citizens of the United States, or in any way abridged, except for participation in rebellion, or other crime, the basis of representation therein shall be reduced in the proportion which the number of such male citizens shall bear to the whole number of male citizens twenty-one years of age in such State.

Section 3. No person shall be a Senator or Representative in Congress, or elector of President and Vice President, or hold

any office, civil or military, under the United States, or under any State, who, having previously taken an oath, as a member of Congress, or as an officer of the United States, or as a member of any State legislature, or as an executive or judicial officer of any State, to support the Constitution of the United States, shall have engaged in insurrection or rebellion against the same, or given aid or comfort to the enemies thereof. But Congress may by a vote of two-thirds of each House, remove such disability.

Section 4. The validity of the public debt of the United States, authorized by law, including debts incurred for payment of pensions and bounties for services in suppressing insurrection or rebellion, shall not be questioned. But neither the United States nor any State shall assume or pay any debt or obligation incurred in aid of insurrection or rebellion against the United States, or any claim for the loss or emancipation of any slave; but all such debts, obligations and claims shall be held illegal and void.

Section 5. The Congress shall have power to enforce, by appropriate legislation, the provisions of this article.

Amendment XV.*

Section 1. The right of citizens of the United States to vote shall not be denied or abridged by the United States or by any State on account of race, color or previous condition of servitude.

Section 2. The Congress shall have power to enforce this article by appropriate legislation.

Amendment XVI.**

The Congress shall have power to lay and collect taxes on incomes, from whatever source derived, without apportionment among the several States, and without regard to any census or enumeration.

Amendment XVII.***

The Senate of the United States shall be composed of two Senators from each State, elected by the people thereof, for six years; and each Senator shall have one vote. The electors in each State shall have the qualifications requisite for electors of the most numerous branch of the State legislatures.

When vacancies happen in the representation of any State in the Senate, the executive authority of such State shall issue writs of election to fill such vacancies: *Provided,* That the legislature of any State may empower the executive thereof to make temporary appointments until the people fill the vacancies by election as the legislature may direct.

This amendment shall not be so construed as to affect the election or term of any Senator chosen before it becomes valid as part of the Constitution.

Amendment XVIII.****

[**Section 1.** After one year from the ratification of this article the manufacture, sale, or transportation of intoxicating liquors

*The Eleventh Amendment was ratified February 7, 1795.
**The Twelfth Amendment as ratified June 15, 1804.

*Superseded by section 3 of the Twentieth Amendment.
**The Thirteenth Amendment was ratified December 6, 1865.
***The Fourteenth Amendment was ratified July 9, 1868.

*The Fifteenth Amendment was ratified February 3, 1870.
**The Sixteenth Amendment was ratified February 3, 1913.
***The Seventeenth Amendment was ratified April 8, 1913.
****The Eighteenth Amendment was ratified January 16, 1919. It was repealed by the Twenty-First Amendment, December 5, 1933.

within, the importation thereof into, or the exportation thereof from the United States and all territory subject to the jurisdiction thereof for beverage purposes is hereby prohibited.

Section 2. The Congress and the several States shall have concurrent power to enforce this article by appropriate legislation.

Section 3. This article shall be inoperative unless it shall have been ratified as an amendment to the Constitution by the legislatures of the several States, as provided in the Constitution, within seven years from the date of the submission hereof to the States by the Congress.]

Amendment XIX.*

The right of citizens of the United States to vote shall not be denied or abridged by the United States or by any State on account of sex.

Congress shall have power to enforce this article by appropriate legislation.

Amendment XX.**

Section 1. The terms of the President and Vice President shall end at noon on the 20th day of January, and the terms of Senators and Representatives at noon on the 3d day of January, of the years in which such terms would have ended if this article had not been ratified; and the terms of their successors shall then begin.

Section 2. The Congress shall assemble at least once in every year and such meeting shall begin at noon on the 3d day of January unless they shall by law appoint a different day.

Section 3. If, at the time fixed for the beginning of the term of the President, the President elect shall have died, the Vice President elect shall become President. If a President shall not have been chosen before the time fixed for the beginning of his term, or if the President elect shall have failed to qualify, then the Vice President elect shall act as President until a President shall have qualified; and the Congress may by law provide for the case wherein neither a President elect nor a Vice President elect shall have qualified, declaring who shall then act as President, or the manner in which one who is to act shall be selected, and such person shall act accordingly until a President or Vice President shall have qualified.

Section 4. The Congress may by law provide for the case of the death of any of the persons from whom the House of Representatives may choose a President whenever the right of choice shall have devolved upon them, and for the case of the death of any of the persons from whom the Senate may choose a Vice President whenever the right of choice shall have devolved upon them.

Section 5. Sections 1 and 2 shall take effect on the 15th day of October following the ratification of this article.

Section 6. This article shall be inoperative unless it shall have been ratified as an amendment to the Constitution by the legislatures of three-fourths of the several States within seven years from the date of its submission.

*The Nineteenth Amendment was ratified August 18, 1920.
**The Twentieth Amendment was ratified January 23, 1933.

Amendment XXI.*

Section 1. The eighteenth article of amendment to the Constitution of the United States is hereby repealed.

Section 2. The transportation or importation into any State, Territory, or possession of the United States for delivery or use therein of intoxicating liquors, in violation of the laws thereof, is hereby prohibited.

Section 3. This article shall be inoperative unless it shall have been ratified as an amendment to the Constitution by conventions in the several States, as provided in the Constitution, within seven years from the date of the submission hereof to the States by the Congress.

Amendment XXII**

Section 1. No person shall be elected to the office of the President more than twice, and no person who has held the office of President, or acted as President, for more than two years of a term to which some other person was elected President shall be elected to the office of the President more than once. But this Article shall not apply to any person holding the office of President when this Article was proposed by the Congress, and shall not prevent any person who may be holding the office of President, or acting as President, during the term within which this Article becomes operative from holding the office of President or acting as President during the remainder of such term.

Section 2. This article shall be inoperative unless it shall have been ratified as an amendment to the Constitution by the legislatures of three-fourths of the several States within seven years from the date of its submission to the States by the Congress.

Amendment XXIII.***

Section 1. The District constituting the seat of Government of the United States shall appoint in such manner as the Congress may direct:

A number of electors of President and Vice President equal to the whole number of Senators and Representatives in Congress to which the District would be entitled if it were a State, but in no event more than the least populous State; they shall be in addition to those appointed by the States, but they shall be considered, for the purposes of the election of President and Vice President, to be electors appointed by a State; and they shall meet in the District and perform such duties as provided by the twelfth article of amendment.

Section 2. The Congress shall have power to enforce this article by appropriate legislation.

Amendment XXIV.****

Section 1. The right of citizens of the United States to vote in any primary or other election for President or Vice President, for electors for President or Vice President, or for Senator or Representative in Congress, shall not be denied or abridged

*The Twenty-First Amendment was ratified December 5, 1933.
**The Twenty-Second Amendment was ratified February 27, 1951.
***The Twenty-Third Amendment was ratified March 29, 1961.
****The Twenty-Fourth Amendment was ratified January 23, 1964.

by the United States or any State by reason of failure to pay any poll tax or other tax.

Section 2. The Congress shall have power to enforce this article by appropriate legislation.

Amendment XXV.*

Section 1. In case of the removal of the President from office or of his death or resignation, the Vice President shall become President.

Section 2. Whenever there is a vacancy in the office of the Vice President, the President shall nominate a Vice President who shall take office upon confirmation by a majority vote of both Houses of Congress.

Section 3. Whenever the President transmits to the President pro tempore of the Senate and the Speaker of the House of Representatives his written declaration that he is unable to discharge the powers and duties of his office, and until he transmits to them a written declaration to the contrary, such powers and duties shall be discharged by the Vice President as Acting President.

Section 4. Whenever the Vice President and a majority of either the principal officers of the executive departments or of such other body as Congress may by law provide, transmit to the President pro tempore of the Senate and the Speaker of the House of Representatives their written declaration that the President is unable to discharge the powers and duties of his office, the Vice President shall immediately assume the powers and duties of the office as Acting President.

Thereafter, when the President transmits to the President pro tempore of the Senate and the Speaker of the House of Representatives his written declaration that no inability exists, he shall resume the powers and duties of his office unless the Vice President and a majority of either the principal officers of the executive department or of such other body as Congress may by law provide, transmit within four days to the President pro tempore of the Senate and the Speaker of the House of Representatives their written declaration that the President is unable to discharge the powers and duties of his office. Thereupon Congress shall decide the issue, assembling within forty-eight hours for that purpose if not in session. If the Congress, within twenty-one days after receipt of the latter written declaration, or, if Congress is not in session, within twenty-one days after Congress is required to assemble, determines by two-thirds vote of both Houses that the President is unable to discharge the powers and duties of his office, the Vice President shall continue to discharge the same as Acting President; otherwise, the President shall resume the powers and duties of his office.

Amendment XXVI.**

Section 1. The right of citizens of the United States, who are eighteen years of age or older, to vote shall not be denied or abridged by the United States or by any State on account of age.

Section 2. The Congress shall have power to enforce this article by appropriate legislation.

*The Twenty-Fifth Amendment was ratified February 10, 1967.
**The Twenty-Sixth Amendment was ratified July 1, 1971.

BICENTENNIAL
MINUTE

Editor's Note: *From January 1987 through September, the* State Bar News *published a column devoted to the bicentennial of the United States Constitution.*

Topics for this "Bicentennial Minute" were selected and written by members of the Association's Committee on Federal Constitution, chaired by Nicole Gordon of New York City. The project was organized by Sheldon Siporin of Brooklyn, whose column on the Articles of Confederation began the series.

In 1788, the United States Constitution was ratified by the state of New York at the Dutchess County Courthouse in Poughkeepsie. A drawing of that courthouse serves as the logo for this column. The drawing was rendered by Albany artist Kimberly Smith, based upon surviving maps and drawings of the building as it looked at the time of ratification.

A crude drawing of the courthouse appeared on the original Dutchess County turnpike map of 1804, now preserved in the county record's room, and reproduced in a 1983 publication called "Dutchess County—a Pictorial History" by John and Mary Jeanneny.

Although the turnpike map drawing has been reproduced many times as the best likeness of the courthouse, the Jeannenys say in their book, "it seems unlikely that the artist took the trouble to accurately reproduce the building which must have been familiar to him. The courthouse shown seems far too small to have housed the 65 delegates of the ratifying convention, plus their aides and the spectators."

Photographs supplied by the Adriance Memorial Library in Poughkeepsie of a tracing made by Henry Booth in 1896 depict the courthouse as having a window over the door on the narrow end of the building and five windows on the long end of the building. The tracing was made from a map drawn by John Beadle in 1802, according to Myra Morales, local historian for the library.

Construction of the Dutchess County Courthouse was completed in 1787. The Ratification Convention for New York State took place in the courthouse in 1788, presided over by Governor George Clinton.

Why Poughkeepsie?

For one, Poughkeepsie was Clinton's hometown and his base of power, said New York City attorney Robert Hendrickson, a member of the Association's Committee on Federal Constitution and author of a critically acclaimed biography on Alexander Hamilton.

Clinton wanted the site of the Ratification Convention away from New York City in order to minimize the influence of the city merchants under Alexander Hamilton who favored the federal Constitution, said Hendrickson. Clinton and the upstate people in general were opposed to it.

The state Legislature was meeting alternately in Albany and New York City at the time. But supporters of the federal Constitution were successful in removing the decision on ratification from the state legislatures, whose members would be reluctant to relinquish any of their sovereignty, said Hendrickson.

At first, the Anti-Federalists in New York appeared to have the majority, but in the eleventh hour, key Anti-Federalists shifted their position, and the Constitution was ratified by a vote of 30 to 27.

(The story of that drama is depicted in a television film called "An Empire of Reason" produced under the auspices of The New York Bar Foundation and The New York State Commission on the Bicentennial of the U.S. Constitution).

The courthouse that housed the Ratification Convention was destroyed by fire in 1806 and replaced by a larger structure, which was, in turn, torn down in 1903, according to the Jeannenys' book.

"No trace remains today of the old courthouse which housed the Ratifying Convention of 1788, and there has been considerable speculation as to how it looked," according to "Dutchess County—a Pictorial History."

Portrait of George Clinton, 1814, by Ezra Ames. Collection of The New-York Historical Society.

George Clinton built a powerful political career in New York during the Revolutionary crisis. Beginning in 1777, he captured the Governor's chair for seven consecutive terms. In 1787-1788, Clinton wielded his political machine and his own pen in a mighty campaign to defeat the Constitution. Writing as "Cato," Clinton sent seven essays to New York newspapers, to be rebuked by the penman "Caesar," in reality Alexander Hamilton. Political ambition outweighed principle, and once the Constitution was ratified, Clinton struggled to be identified with the winning cause and its greatest hero, George Washington. In 1789, Clinton won the governorship again, successfully branding his opponent as an enemy of the new federal government.

From September 15-17, 1887, Philadelphia was the site of the Centennial Celebration of the Constitution.

Sixteen of the 38 states and the District of Columbia sent representatives to attend the three-day gala. Several hundred thousand on-lookers lined the nine-mile processional route. The program pictured was printed to commemorate the occasion and contained a copy of the Constitution as well as biographies of the Founding Fathers.

The holiday ended with a speech by President Grover Cleveland, who was a member of the New York State Bar Association, and a rally in Independence Square.

Congress, State Sovereignty & the Articles of Confederation

by Sheldon Siporin, Esq.

The recent report of the Federalism Working Group replays the political dissonances which resounded throughout the birth of our federal Republic. A reprise of the past in this bicentennial year provides a measure of perspective.

The chartered British colonies in America in the 1760s were not a harmonious band. The first notes of unity rang out in response to the so-called Intolerable Acts of Parliament. The Stamp Act of 1765, which required stamps to be attached to all legal documents, was an early tyrannical imposition. The individually weak colonies began to act in concert. Representatives of nine colonies met in New York on October 7, 1765, and composed a "Declaration of Rights and Grievances against the King." This Stamp Act Congress set the tone for joint resistance to oppression and led to the creation of quasi-revolutionary "committees of correspondance" to promote intercolonial cooperation.

The dominant theme of colonial actions against the Crown was the principle of "state sovereignty" overlaid on a background of individual rights. Patrick Henry declared that the rights of Englishmen included the right to be governed by their local assemblies "in the article of taxes and internal police." The Declaration of Rights and Grievances asserted that only the colonial legislatures could lawfully impose taxes.

The British Parliament reacted much as the present federal government would to a blanket refusal of New Yorkers to pay federal income or excise tax: troops were dispatched to chastise the radicals and quell protest. This set off colonial provocations such as the Boston Tea Party. The British navy then shut down Boston Harbor in May 1774.

This sounded an alarm to other colonies along the eastern seaboard. New York and Philadelphia took the lead in conducting a "general congress" of all the colonies to warn the redcoats that an "attack upon one colony is an attack upon all." Early calls for nationhood struck some common chords but faded in the clamor for reconciliation with the Crown. There was still no clear concept of extracolonial authority or central government.

The general Congress resolved that, if there was no redress of grievance by May 10, 1775, a further Congress would be held. John Hancock was selected as president of the Congress and a skeletal bureaucracy was set up to negotiate with the Crown. British disdain and increasing militancy resulted in the bloodbaths known as Lexington and Concord. The revolution was being played to a crescendo.

The Second Continental Congress assembled in May 1775 to "put the colonies in a state of defense." New York and Connecticut were requested to send forces to fortify the forts in Lake Champlain after the takeover of Fort Ticonderoga by guerilla troops under Ethan Allan.

The Continental Congresses were assemblages of exigency and extremity. Theories of federalism and state sovereignty were mere static in the melody of revolution. Central Congressional direction of the timbre and tempo of resistance was pure practicality. By necessity a precursor government arose. Appropriate administrative instrumentality was designed. A committee was appointed to borrow money for powder and guns for the colonial armies.

Quotas were set for the raising of companies of riflemen. George Washington was chosen to command the United Continental forces. Support staff and wage scales were set. Each colony state insisted on its sovereign pre-eminence and on its sovereign right to a quota of generals. New York, always a major player in the colonial symphony, was accorded a major general: Philip Schuyler. Benjamin Franklin, eternally one beat beyond his peers, composed a draft "Articles of Confederation and Perpetual Union," which was initially tabled.

Congress continued to assume increased power along with obligation. An army runs on money, which was in short supply. Gouverneur Morris of New York made a pitch to permit the printing of paper currency by Congress. This plan, promoted by James

Duane, a New York representative in Congress, was adopted, and the legendary "continental money" was issued. Congress, which to some minds was insidiously amassing power, was still a function of expediency. It lacked the power of taxation and had no enforcement capability as the states were covetous of their prerogatives.

At last in 1776, prodded by a Virginia resolution that "these United Colonies are, and of right ought to be, free and independent states," Congress declared independence from Britain. This purportedly "formalized" the existing situation. It also would facilitate alliances with friendly foreign powers, such as France, and solidify union. The colony states continued to believe that common cause was not repugnant to individual sovereignty.

A formal plan for confederation was prepared along with the Declaration of Independence. John Dickinson of Pennsylvania was assigned primary responsibility to write the score for national governance. Meanwhile, a committee was selected to draft a "plan of Treaties" with foreign powers.

The plan of confederation was a bitter source of discord. Each state, given the chance, preferred to perform in solo. States' rightists then as now sought local autonomy and feared the ostensible tyranny of central authority. Thus, Dickinson's draft, which culled stanzas from Franklin's grand composition, unsettled many representatives. Congress appeared to be granted formidable powers: control over relations with foreign countries, war and peace, coining and borrowing money, disputes between the states, trade and relations with the Indians, and postal communications. That these powers were already de facto was ignored.

Thomas Burke, a representative from South Carolina, warned that the draft contained only the express reservation of police power to the states without any clear limitation on congressional power. He feared this constituted an implicit resignation of all other state power; it might permit a future Congress to "explain away every right belonging to the states and to make their own power as unlimited as they please." The modern Charles Coopers are strong parallels to the Thomas Burkes of the colonial age, all playing their parts in the orchestration of the democratic Republic.

A revised draft of the Articles explicitly stated the sovereignty of the several states:

Each state retains its sovereignty, freedome and independence, and every power, jurisdiction and right which is not by this confederation expressly delegated to the United States in Congress assembled.

The proposed confederation was termed a "League of friendship" and a "mutual defense pact". Still, many states were reluctant to accept even the diluted document.

There were several counternotes struck in the colonial concert. The colonies sought alliance with France, an objective promoting union since, even combined, the colonial contingent massed merely the populace of modern Brooklyn, hardly inspiring. Border disputes disrupted intercolonial relations. Some colonial charters granted sovereignty to the Pacific Ocean. Colonies without such claims feared these "landed" colonies, and wanted western territory under joint, congressional control. (John Jay believed that the western territories were simply too vast for anything other than joint control.) The war with Britain still had to be won, which required congressional direction.

New York State confronted New Hampshire over ownership of land along the Connecticut River (latter day Vermont). New York also laid claim to western lands. Meanwhile, several New England states opposed New York General Schuyler's command of the northern continental armies.

New York in its self-interest, leaned in favor of confederation and central government. Thus, in February 1780, the New York Legislature, prompted by Schuyler, adopted a resolution which ceded New York's claim to the western territory. This encouraged other "landed" states to follow its lead and smooth the path to confederation. New York also hoped that its gesture would reinforce its remaining claims to Vermont.

In October 1780, New York made the strongest statement in favor of Congress and resolved:

That Congress should during the war or until a perpetual confederation shall be completed, exercise every power which they may deem necessary for an effectual prosecution of the war.

This included the power to compel any state by military force to furnish its quota of men, money and provisions for the war effort. Such language shocked the other colonies.

Pressure of circumstances forced most of the colonies to adopt the Articles of Confederation in 1781. Congressional control over the western territories made the Congress a true supracolonial authority, though still lacking the complete requisites of national government. New York itself hedged its adoption of the Articles by making it contingent on adoption by all other colonies. Maryland, the last holdout, finally adopted the Articles in February 1781 when the French ambassador refused to provide protection against the British navy in Chesapeake Bay until ratification was complete. The Articles of Confederation formally took effect on March 1, 1781. A critical key to the hymn of the Republic had been found.

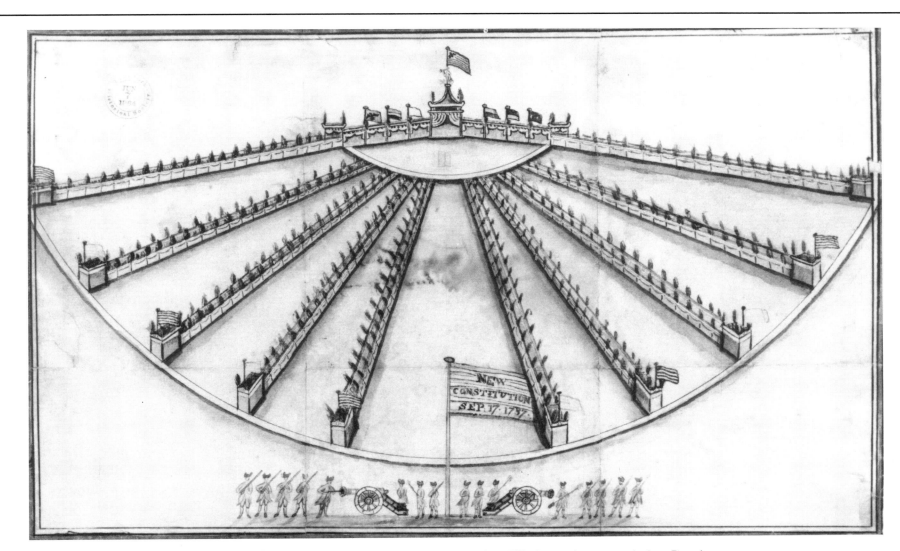

David Grim. Banquet Pavilion, undated. Water-color on paper. Gift of Sophia Minton, 1864.17.

New York City gave a huge party on July 23, 1788, celebrating the nation's new Constitution. This watercolor depicts the Banquet Pavilion erected for the celebration. The Pavilion was designed by Major Charles *Pierre L'Enfant and was erected where Broadway and Broome Street now intersect. Ten tables were arranged in a rising sun pattern to represent the ten states that had already ratified the U.S. Constitution and to accommodate the five thousand marchers who turned out that day.*

In 1784, three years before the Constitution was ultimately ratified, a group later known as the Federalists launched a campaign to increase the powers of the central government.

Up to then, the Articles of Confederation granted authority to each of the states to collect taxes, issue currency and maintain its own army. The central government, such as it was, primarily concerned itself with foreign relations and treaties. The president was merely a figurehead.

It was a time when the economic outlook was bleak; The Continental Congress had a "national" war debt of approximately $42 million (some quick math would make that the 1980s equivalent of more than $20 billion) without a means to raise revenues.

A pro-nationalist engraver named Amos Doolittle of Connecticut created this illustration, which depicts the Federalists under a shining sun while their rivals congregate under storm clouds. Other symbols may be less apparent, but the key points are easily identifiable — pensions for war veterans, the issuing of inflationary paper currency, and a burdensome, crazy-quilt system of taxes.

Alexandre Roslin. *Benjamin Franklin,* ca. 1789-1790 (after Joseph S. Duplessis). Oil on canvas. The Louis Dorr Fund. 1892.8.

Benjamin Franklin, renowned in Europe and America for his achievements in science, art, literature and public service, and at eighty-one the oldest delegate, declared the Convention "the most august and respectable Assembly" he was ever in in his life.

BICENTENNIAL MINUTE

The Federalist Papers: The New York Bar's Great Gift to "We the People"

by Robert A. Hendrickson, Esq.

After reading the 85 Federalist Papers as they were published one by one from October 1787 to May 1788, George Washington, who would take office 10 months later as the first president under the new Constitution, wrote his former aide, Alexander Hamilton, what for Washington amounted to a rave review:

"I have read every performance which has been printed on one side and the other of the great question lately agitated ... perusal of the political papers under the signature of Publius has afforded me great satisfaction ... without an unmeaning compliment, I will say that I have seen no other so well calculated to produce conviction in an unbiased mind, as the Production of your Triumvirate."

Thomas Jefferson, then congress' minister in Paris, and soon to become the first Secretary of State and mortal antagonist of Hamilton, the first Secretary of the Treasury, warmly commended *The Federalist* to James Madison, the third member of the Publius Triumvirate, as "the best commentary on the principles of government ever written."

Young James Kent, later New York's Chancellor, identifying Hamilton as chief author, wrote that as "ingenious and political research," it is "not inferior to Gibbon, Hume and Montesquieu." Guizot, the sage French foreign minister, later wrote, "in the application of elementary principles of government to practical administration, it was the greatest work known" to him.

And a century and a half later the great populist historian Charles A. Beard called *The Federalist* "the most instructive work on political science ever written in the United States; and owing to its practical character it ranks first in the world's literature of that subject." After two centuries, at its Bicentennial this year, *The Federalist,* and these appraisals of it

by Washington, Jefferson, Guizot, Chancellor Kent and Charles Beard, and countless other experts of every sort, remain unchallenged. Like its subject, the Constitution, *The Federalist* stands as a pinnacle of political thought that is perceived as ever great and more prescient as time and change roll on and its third century begins.

In the narrowest sense, *The Federalist* is a collection of 85 essays first published as articles simultaneously in four of the five New York City newspapers every two or three days beginning October 27, 1787, five weeks after the Constitutional Convention in Philadelphia had adjourned, and ending May 28, 1788, three weeks before New York State's constitutional ratifying convention would convene in Poughkeepsie. It was addressed to the "People of the State of New York." Four states were crucial to the success of any new government—Pennsylvania, Massachusetts, Virginia and New York—and New York was the key state; but nowhere was opposition stronger.

Hamilton, who had been New York's most active delegate to the Philadelphia Convention, and an active member of the Continental Congress under the Articles of Confederation, which convened in New York, conceived the idea and made the decision to write and publish the essays. Their purpose was to defend the new Constitution, to explain the meaning of its provisions, and to respond to the many articles by Anti-Federalists and others denouncing it which were then appearing in newspapers not only in New York, but throughout the 13 states. Typical were those under the pen name of "Cato", by New York's powerful Governor George Clinton, who led New York's opposition to the Constitution.

Hamilton, a leading member of the New York bar, first enlisted his older friend and mentor John Jay, another leading member of the New York bar and also an alumnus of King's College, later Columbia, to be his collaborator. Jay was soon to become the first Chief Justice of the new United States Supreme Court, whose constitutional powers *The Federal-*

ist Papers, particularly in No. 78 by Hamilton, would powerfully reinforce. Hamilton also asked Gouverneur Morris, another leading New York lawyer to contribute, but he declined the invitation to immortality. James Madison, the third member of the Publius Triumvirate, like Hamilton had been a leading member of the Philadelphia convention. As a member of the soon-to-be superseded Continental Congress, he was in New York attending its last sessions in the de facto capital, which would soon become the first official capital of the United States under "We the People of the United States of America."

Hamilton outlined the whole series and assigned parts to Madison and Jay. The name "Publius," a prize-winning mime of Roman times which Hamilton had used earlier for public papers, was appropriate to conceal the names of three collaborators writing as one—a prize-winning mime could switch seamlessly from one identity to another in the course of a single performance. Jay wrote numbers 2 through 5 dealing with foreign affairs, but was wounded in a street riot, and returned to write only No. 64, on the Senate's role in the treaty-making process. Madison wrote numbers 10, 14, 37 through 48 and 53. Both Madison and Hamilton later claimed authorship of the other numbers. Disputation has raged among their respective champions ever since, as in their later lives, over authorship of 49 through 58, 62 and 63, which Hamilton probably outlined or co-wrote with Madison. Hamilton wrote all the rest, a total of about 50 of the 85. The signature *Publius* for the whole series kept the attention of the readers focused on the points being made rather than on the personalities—and peccadilloes—of the well known individual advocates.

Hamilton's overall plan of composition was probably not plainly visible to Madison and Jay or newspaper readers from the beginning. But as the series unfolded from its methodical analysis of the clauses and sections of the Constitution, there emerged a coherent statement of the nature and purposes of all government, and a universal political philosophy for a government of freedom under law adapted to the American setting.

Hamilton would write in haste, late at night, by candlelight, at home, or in scraps of time between clients in his busy Wall Street law office, or during lulls in Congress' sessions held at the corner of Broad and Wall Streets, where Federal Hall now stands. His wife, Elizabeth, after the children were in bed, would make copies of his drafts in her own hand as the pages filled up with neat script from his racing pen. They would deliver them to the waiting printer who would sometimes catch the sheets unsanded to rush them into galleys to meet each new deadline as it passed, two or three or four times a week for six months.

But had the Publius Triumvirate planned and brooded for years before setting down the first words on paper, the three busy men could hardly have created a more unified architectonic literary structure. The stately, magisterial, serene tone that *The Federalist,* No. 1 by Hamilton, set for the whole series lends credibility to the tradition that he wrote it while sitting on the deck of a sloop sailing up the Hudson for one of his numerous court appearances in Albany:

> *"You are called upon to deliberate on a New Constitution for the United States of America. The subject speaks its own importance; comprehending in its consequences, nothing less than the existence of the UNION, the safety and welfare of the parts of which it is composed, the fate of an empire, in many respects the most interesting in the world. It has been frequently remarked, that it seems to have been reserved to the people of this country, by their conduct and example, to decide the important question, whether societies of men are really capable or not, of establishing good government from reflection and choice, or whether they are forever destined to depend, for their political constitutions, on accident and force."*

So begins *The Federalist Papers,* the gift of two great members of the New York bar (with a strong assist from Virginia counsel) to "We the People of the United States of America," and our troubled world—where no more perfect union than Publius' establishing freedom under law has yet been explicated, and put into practical effect.

The Federalist also accomplished its immediate purpose: its eloquent arguments helped to turn around the New York and Virginia ratifying conventions, where strong majorities led by George Clinton and Patrick Henry, respectively, which had initially opposed the Constitution, came around to it in the end. Only thereby was the new Constitution by its own terms formally put into practical effect.

Joseph Wright. *John Jay,* 1786. Oil on canvas. Gift of John Pintard, 1817.5.

John Jay ardently supported the movement for a stronger central government. Because New York politics was dominated by the anti-nationalist Governor George Clinton and his followers, Jay was not named to the delegation that went to Philadelphia in 1787. He campaigned tirelessly for ratification, writing pamphlets, attending the state convention at Poughkeepsie, and contributing five essays to The Federalist.

When the new government was organized, President Washington appointed John Jay to be the first Chief Justice of the Supreme Court. The position carries more prestige now than in the nation's earliest years. While serving on the bench, Jay ran unsuccessfully for elected office and accepted a diplomatic mission to Great Britain. Finally, he resigned from the fledgling court in 1796 to take a more important job, as Governor of New York.

John Jay's original manuscript for *The Federalist*
Number 64.

*This essay, in the handwriting of John Jay, was
discovered in a box of Jay family papers at The New-
York Historical Society in 1959. The whereabouts
of only one other original* Federalist *essay is known,
Number 5 by John Jay in the archives of Columbia
University. None of the original essays by Madison
or Hamilton has survived.*

*Of the five essays written by John Jay, Number 64
is especially interesting in our time. Jay explained
the framers' decision to entrust the negotiation of
treaties to the President, rather than Congress. Foreign Affairs requires "perfect* secrecy *and immediate
dispatch," he argued. "The convention have done
well, therefore, in so disposing of the power of making treaties that although the President must, in
forming them, act by the advice and consent of the Senate, yet he will be able to manage the business of intel-
ligence in such manner as prudence may suggest."*

John Trumbull. *Alexander Hamilton,* after 1840. Oil on canvas. Gift of Thomas J. Bryan, 1867.305.

As soon as the Constitutional Convention unveiled the new plan of government, Alexander Hamilton hurried home to wage a long, arduous battle for ratification in New York State. There, Governor George Clinton was already mounting a formidable campaign against the Constitution. Hamilton and John Jay recruited James Madison to join them in writing eighty-five essays in defense of the Constitution under the pseudonym "Publius." This amazing literary effort, conceived in crisis and scribbled in haste, became the enduring, authoritative treatise on the Constitution.

In Federalist No. 78, Hamilton rebutted the Anti-Federalists' claim that judicial review would give the judges an arbitrary, uncontrollable power. It was the court's duty to strike down any law that conflicted with the Constitution, which was the fundamental expression of "the intention of the people." Hamilton insisted that judges would not have the authority to substitute "their own pleasure" for the decisions made by the legislators.

BICENTENNIAL
MINUTE

The Articles of Confederation as Forerunner of the Union

by the Honorable Dominic R. Massaro

Up to 1787, governmental operations were conducted by the Second Continental Congress. This, on a tentative basis at best, without the stability of an instrument that delegated real power to it. It was an extralegal body, born of necessity and accepted because of the exigencies of the war. It served reasonably well the needs of the time so long as enthusiasm for the Revolution was extant. And even in this space of its activity, it had been quite inefficient in securing the means of feeding, clothing and paying the army. Indeed, throughout the war it was compelled to resort to expedients which were entirely at variance with strict adherence to public faith, and in whatever it did, it was compelled to wait upon the oftentimes tardy assent of 13 distinct legislative bodies.

In particular, its neglect of the army was not only scandalous but highly dangerous. With the war all but ended, the officers, ignoring Congress, called upon Washington to take the initiative and proclaim himself dictator. Had he chosen to play the part, Washington might well have established a constitutional monarchy. He not only rejected the appeal, but suppressed the movement and by his firmness and patriotism prevented civil war. But the appeal had its effect. If it did not reveal the temper of the army, it certainly pointed to the weakness of the government.

True, there were the Articles of Confederation. Drafted by a committee of the Congress in eight days in 1776, the necessity of unanimous state action withheld final approval for five years, until March 1, 1781. Professing to be articles of perpetual union, Congress had no power to effect or maintain union.

This was reflected in the Articles themselves which provided: "Each State retains its sovereignty, freedome and independence." Another provision stated: "The said states hereby severally enter into a firm league of friendship with each other."

A "firm league" to carry on war against the British Empire. These were states speaking to each other in terms traditionally reserved to independent nations.

And the sovereignty and equality of the 13 states were fully preserved by equal voting power in the Congress—one state, one vote, irrespective of size or population. In all these respects sharp changes were to be made by the Constitution within the decade.

Vested interests

Loosely bound to each other by the Articles, then, each state was ruled by governments closely responding to vested property interests. The Dutch land grantees and importing merchants of New York are a striking example.

Young as they were, the states had a background in colonial administration which entrenched the dominant groups in most of them beyond the apparent possibility of displacement by electoral means. But battering upon them, more particularly from New Hampshire to Maryland, was a menacing, immeasurable force, arising from the soil and, to a limited degree, from the forge and workshop. Men untrained in politics, ignorant of the niceties of public finance, but woefully aware of their debts and the specter of debtors' prison, were hurling themselves upon state legislatures, demanding and securing the issuance of paper money unbacked by specie, demanding the right to pay farm mortgages in installments, crying for laws that would limit debt vis-a-vis the time-honored system of foreclosure and imprisonment. There arose a huge outcry against all who had money and ease and comfort.

Congress is government

The entire national government consisted of just one agency: a Congress, at that moment sitting upstairs in New York's City Hall. Philadelphia, Baltimore, Lancaster, York, Princeton, Annapolis, Trenton—all had been home to the Continental Congress over the years as it was chased from pillar

to post by war or, in one instance, by mutinying ill-paid soldiers of the Pennsylvania militia. It was a wandering council without strong national sentiment. There was no president, no cabinet, no courts, not even a bicameral Congress at that! To meet annually, it consisted of a single house. While each state had one vote, it could be represented by from two to seven delegates selected as the legislature of that state might direct. In practice these were commonly selected by the state legislature itself, subject to its control and recall, and paid in such sums as it fixed.

Given the fact that state finances were not in a flourishing condition, there were seldom more than two delegates from any one state present at the sessions of Congress, while at times some of the states were entirely unrepresented. Often during the war, when Congress should have had 91 members, hardly 25 were present, and on more than one occasion Congress was compelled to adjourn for days at a time because there was no quorum. Since the war ended, it had been difficult to obtain a quorum. Members simply stayed home, preferring state interests to the general government.

Even when, in 1783, Washington presented his resignation as Commander-in-Chief, there were but 20 delegates present, representing seven states.

Fundamentally, on paper at least, Congress possessed all the power delegated to a central government: it was, at once, legislative, executive and judiciary. Yet it lacked compulsory authority either to enforce its actions or punish for failure to comply with its dictates. The system provided no separation of powers: Congress, as a deliberative body, adopted policies and then, through committees of its own members or agents selected by it, attempted to carry them out.

A presiding officer, called a president, was elected annually by the Congress. He was in no sense a national chief executive. Inasmuch as the body was not in continuous session and some central officer was required to be continuously at the seat of government, nominally in Philadelphia, a "Committee

33

of States," consisting of one member from each state delegation, was selected to act during the interim(s).

The only judicial work envisioned for the central government by those who framed the Articles, and, indeed, the only such work as could arise under the system they created, was the settlement of disputes between two or more states. This responsibility was also delegated to the Congress. When such occasions arose, special tribunals or commissions were empowered to decide the controversy. But in such cases, as in all other matters, the Congress lacked power to enforce the decisions if the parties to the dispute did not willingly accept the outcome.

Weakness of confederation

Justice Story, in his *Commentaries,* points out the inherent defects of the Confederation in those matters which Congress had reference in answering the design and necessities of a national government:

They may make and conclude treaties, but can only record the observances of them. They may appoint ambassadors, but cannot even defray the expenses of their tables. They may borrow money in their own name, on the faith of the union, but cannot pay a dollar. They may coin money, but they cannot purchase an ounce of bullion. They may make war, and determine what number of troups are necessary, but cannot raise a single soldier. In short, they may declare everything, but do nothing.

Clearly, it is almost incorrect to call the Continental Congress a "government," for it lacked real compulsory authority. Its actions were not laws; they were resolutions or requisitions.

Measured by the governmental structure fashioned later under the Constitution, the national machinery was a model of simplicity more concerned with protecting 13 separate interests than in meeting the needs of nationhood.

Indeed, as Madison says in reflecting the mind of the majority of the country's national leaders of the day, "the present system neither has nor deserves advocates, and if some very strong props are not applied, will quickly tumble to the ground."

Supporting the move toward a stronger national government were the Eastern commercial interests—men of business who needed uniform trade policies, elimination of state trade barriers and a sound currency system for the successful operation of commerce. Opposed were Western farmers and Southern planters. And the forces of state sovereignty were not to be easily overcome. Nor was it accomplished by, and at the time of, the adoption of the Constitution, as the Civil War would later bear testimony. A truly national consciousness would not evolve in the American psyche until the end of the following century.

Annapolis convention

As early as 1782, the New York Legislature proposed that a convention be held to revise the Articles, but Congress took no action.

At length, in September 1786, in response to a Virginia invitation, five impatient middle states met at Annapolis for a discussion of trade and navigation issues. This "Annapolis Convention," fruitless though it was in solving the problem, was a testimonial to the state of affairs into which the government had fallen, for it was an attempt to do by informal conference what the duly established Congress could not do. Nonetheless, it became the forerunner of the Constitutional Convention. The deliberations resulted in a recommendation that all the states be requested to send delegates to a convention at Philadelphia the following spring to consider the Articles of Confederation and propose such changes therein as might render them adequate to the exigencies of the Union.

Congress looked rather doubtfully upon this movement. It was questionable whether any suggested changes would be constitutional unless they originated in Congress itself, and were then submitted to and adopted by the various state legislatures in accordance with the Articles.

Shays' Rebellion

It can hardly be doubted that the action of Congress and of the several states regarding the convention call was hastened by an alarming condition in Massachusetts, an insurrection!

Like other states, Massachusetts was burdened with heavy debt at the close of the war. Everybody was in debt, money was scarce. Discontent prevailed, particularly in the rural communities.

The principles of finance were scarcely known to the fairly well informed, and were wholly missed by the mass of the population, that now demanded a reorganization of the state government favorable to debtors. Proceeding from inflammatory words of action, the spirit of lawlessness broke out under the leadership of Daniel Shays, in the late fall of 1786. For four months, the insurrection raged, and was given aid and comfort by the disaffected in surrounding states; and the disaffected were likewise represented in the assemblies of these states. Had it not been for the sagacity of Governor Bowdoin, the outbreak, which has received Shays' name, would have spread over all of New England.

While this chapter is only of collateral interest, the influence of Shays' Rebellion in hastening the Constitutional Convention was very great. Insurrection hinted ominously at a general civil disorganization, for it originated with the people. To say that it frightened Congress and alarmed the friends of law and order everywhere doubtless presents it in its true light as a factor in the formation of the more perfect union. Its attempt, which was for a time successful, to overawe the courts and to defy the laws, might be imitated in other States. Clearly, it turned the tide of sentiment. The delegates would convene at Philadelphia within a season of its suppression.

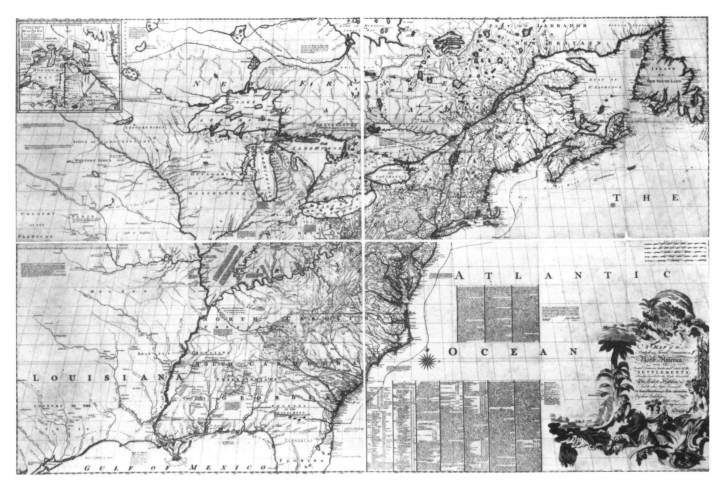

"Map of the British and French Dominions in North America ... ," drawn by John Mitchell in 1755.

In November 1782, John Jay carried this map to Paris to negotiate a treaty with Great Britain ending the War of Independence. On the map Jay marked by hand the boundaries of the new United States.

The American government established by the Articles of Confederation was powerless to compel the states to honor the terms of the Treaty. The states failed to protect loyalists from harsh reprisals and to compel the repayment debts owed to British creditors. In turn, the British refused to honor United States boundaries and evacuate Niagara, Detroit and other garrisons on U.S. soil. In 1786, George Washington told Jay, "Your sentiments, that our affairs are drawing rapidly to a crisis, accord with my own ... If you tell the [state] Legislatures they have violated the treaty of peace and invaded the prerogatives of the Confederacy, they will laugh in your face."

Portrait of John Adams, 1835 by Asher B. Durand.
Collection of The New-York Historical Society.

In December 1786, as the nation prepared for the Constitutional Convention, John Adams published the first volume of his treatise on the principles and structures of good government, "A Defense of the Constitutions of Government of the United States of America." *In the third volume, Adams lavishly praised the Convention "as the greatest single effort of national deliberation that the world has ever seen." The Constitution had shortcomings. But "a people who could conceive and adopt" their own government "we need not fear will be able to amend it, when by experience, its inconveniences and imperfections shall be seen and felt." What merited celebration was the actual inventing.*

Speaker's desk and lectern from the First Congress of the United States. Collection of The New-York Historical Society.

The first House of Representatives convened at Federal Hall in New York City on April 1, 1789. This desk, designed by Major Pierre Charles L'Enfant, was used by the Speaker of the House. A slant-topped lectern supported by an imperious eagle rests on the Sheraton-style desk.

BICENTENNIAL
MINUTE

Liberty and Order: The Lessons of the New York Convention

by Jane H. Hovde, Esq.

Between the signing of the Constitution in Philadelphia on September 17, 1787, and its ratification by New York in July 1788, occurred the first great national debate under an established system of republican governments. The men involved believed they were making a decision not only for themselves but "for millions unborn."

A genuinely radical change was at issue, the sides were about evenly divided, and the contest over ratification was hotly fought, particularly in New York State. In New York, the Anti-Federalists, who opposed the Constitution, were in the majority, and the contest was played out in a context of local partisan politics. To read the repeated charges of "aristocracy" and "tyranny" and "conspiracy" made by the Anti-Federalists during the ratification campaign can easily give the impression that America was on the verge of a class war in 1787-1788 and that the issue was indeed one of liberty or tyranny. Yet the losing side accepted its defeat, not always gracefully perhaps, but it accepted it. This result, which we take for granted today, was by no means assured in 1788.

Country has changed

With our rapid communication and transportation today, it is difficult to imagine the country seen by its inhabitants in 1787. Differences between Maine and Georgia were very great: differences in climate and terrain had produced differences in the economy; economic differences, combined with other contrasts such as religion, had produced significant variations in culture as well. Although Americans shared some basic political beliefs and had "middling classes;" the "great opulent families" no longer controlled the politics of the state as they had in the colony. These new men feared that a frustrated aristocracy was uniting under the banner of the Constitution to achieve the power which had eluded it

since the break with Britain. The battle over ratification in New York was thus a party struggle as well as one between different views of the appropriate government design.

Ideas of the past

In their opposition to the Constitution, the Anti-Federalists relied on the fixed ideas of the past. They represented the inflexible position in the American political tradition, while the Federalists represented a more experimental and empirical approach. Yet in the political resolution of their differences in the New York Convention, both sides demonstrated a pragmatism which became characteristic of American political life.

When the delegates met in Poughkeepsie in June 1788 to consider the Constitution, the Anti-Federalists numerically dominated the Convention 46 to 19 and the situation hardly seemed auspicious for its advocates. By the time the delegates assembled, however, eight states had ratified the Constitution and the conventions of New Hampshire and Virginia were already in progress. While New York debated, these conventions ratified the Constitution, making the new union a fait accompli.

Clause-by-clause debate

Although their ideas logically pointed to outright rejection of the Constitution, the New York Anti-Federalists agreed before the Convention to debate the Constitution clause by clause, and to propose amendments, and "that the Constitution will be effectively amended previous to its adoption—or that it will be totally rejected." By this strategy some Anti-Federalists were hoping that Virginia would reject the Constitution. Others were more confident about working out the desired amendments, and all were avoiding any charge of irresponsibility. Thus the debate began.

The New York Anti-Federalists, like those in other states, believed the adoption of the Constitution,

with its increased centralization of power in the federal government, would endanger the new experiments in republican government in America. This belief stemmed from their conviction, supported by contemporary political thought, that republican government was possible only for a small territory and a homogeneous population. They failed to grasp the meaning of the new federalism and to see the proposed government as one of limited enumerated powers. They saw the new government as a national consolidated government, no longer a federal government as it was under the Articles of Confederation. For did it not have the power to levy taxes directly on individuals and the power to raise and maintain an army, a navy and to call forth and command the militia of the several states. Not only did this make possible the existence of a feared standing army, but it threatened the ability of the state to defend itself by subjecting the citizen militia to national control. And the provision in Article VI making the Constitution and the Laws of the U.S. the supreme law of the land seemed to clearly locate sovereign power in the new central government, not the states. The Anti-Federalists thought that such a national consolidated government would almost certainly abolish the state governments and impose uniform laws upon a diverse people. This could only mean tyranny and the destruction of republican government.

Anti-Federalist theory

Closely connected to the belief that republican government could operate only over a small area was the Anti-Federalists' theory of representation. They regarded representation more as an institutional substitution for direct democracy. The representatives should "resemble those they represent." A legislature should be an exact miniature of the people, containing representatives for all classes, interests and opinions in the community. This was, of course, impossible to achieve in a national congress—there would not be enough seats to go around. Under the

Constitution, constituencies would be large with a ratio of one representative per 30,000 people. The Federalists saw this process of "filtering" public opinion as a virtue since it would serve to discourage factions so endemic in pure democracies and to reconcile different interests to achieve the general good.

The Federalists were concerned with establishing a legislature which would encourage "wise deliberation and vigorous execution" and recognized more clearly the role which compromise must play in popular government. For the Anti-Federalists, a congress thus elected could not truly represent the will of the people, and they particularly feared that they themselves, the "middling class," would be left out, as Melancton Smith, the leading spokesman of the Anti-Federalists at the New York Convention, so eloquently explained. He argued that with the small number of representatives in the House of Representatives "men in the middling class … will not be so anxious to be chosen … the office will be highly elevated and distinguished … [and] render the place of a representative not a desirable one to sensible, substantial men, who have been used to walk in the plain and frugal paths of life."

Defeat certain

Even if they should choose to run for election, they would almost certainly be defeated. In a large electoral district it would be difficult for any but a person of "conspicuous military, popular, civil or legal talents" to win. The great "easily unite their interests: the common people will divide, and their divisions will be promoted by the others. There will be scarcely a chance of their uniting in any other but some great mass unless in some popular demagogue, who will probably be destitute of principle. A substantial yeoman, of sense and discernment, will hardly ever be chosen."

This government would be controlled by the great and would not truly reflect the interests of all groups and would thus be a government of oppression. Given

their profound distrust of the representative and electoral provisions in the proposed Constitution, the Anti-Federalists wanted both an increase in the number of representatives in Congress and more explicit limitations of the central government's powers as well the means to enforce them. They feared exactly what has come to be most admired in the U.S. Constitution—its brevity and its open-ended generality. They wanted an explicitness which would confine the discretion of the government within narrow boundaries. As Smith expressed it: "Matters of moment should not be left to doubtful construction."

Many amendments

The New York Convention produced a ratification document containing 32 amendments to revise the structure of the proposed government, with a preamble enumerating the liberties to be protected in a Bill of Rights. By July 8, the convention had finished its consideration of the Constitution and the debate turned to whether New York ratification should be conditional on the acceptance of these amendments.

By this time the New York delegates knew that New Hampshire and Virginia had ratified the Constitution. That fact, together with the increasing popular opinion in the state in favor of ratification, particularly in the southern counties, and the skillful tactics of the Federalists, caused the Anti-Federalist ranks to break. The Federalists played on the delegates' fears of the consequences of conditional ratification while making offers of conciliation about the amendments. As Smith, in changing his position, warned his colleagues, rejection might cause "convulsions in the southern part" of the state, and "discord in the rest," with the result that their party might be "dispersed like sheep on a mountain." On July 26, New York ratified the Constitution "in full confidence" that a second convention would consider the amendments, and a circular letter was sent to other state legislatures, calling on them to approve a second convention.

Bill of Rights emerges

The Anti-Federalists of New York had lost the contest, but their influence was not ended with their defeat in 1788. Their criticism about the lack of a bill of rights led to the adoption of the first 10 amendments in the first Congress of the new government, and their concern about the dangers of centralized federal power is part of the American political tradition. The Federalists were more open to experiment and perhaps more confident about the ability of America to adapt the Constitution to its evolving needs. But both attitudes are necessary to combine order and efficiency in a government with liberty.

REDEUNT SATURNIA REGNA.

On the erection of the Eleventh PILLAR of the great Na-tional DOME, we beg leave most sincerely to felicitate "OUR DEAR COUNTRY."

Rise it will.

The foundation good—it may yet be saved.

The FEDERAL EDIFICE.

ELEVEN STARS, in quick succession rise—
ELEVEN COLUMNS strike our wond'ring eyes,
Soon o'er the *whole*, shall swell the beauteous DOME,
COLUMBIA's boast—and FREEDOM's hallow'd home.
  Here shall the ARTS in glorious splendour shine !
And AGRICULTURE give her stores divine !
COMMERCE refin'd, dispense us more than gold,
And this new world, teach WISDOM to the old—
RELIGION here shall fix her blest abode,
Array'd in *mildness*, like its parent GOD !
JUSTICE and LAW, shall endless PEACE maintain,
And *the* "SATURNIAN AGE," *return again.*

———

Cartoon from the *Massachusetts Centinel,* August 2, 1788. Collection of The New-York Historical Society.

  When news reached Massachusetts that the Poughkeepsie convention had ratified the Constitution, the Centinel *published this cartoon, celebrating New York as the eleventh pillar of the great national edifice. Similar images, depicting the ratifying states as sturdy neoclassical columns, appeared frequently in newspapers everywhere.*

Thirteen-star United States flag. Hand woven cotton, 26″ x 34″.

American patriots waited almost a year after the Declaration of Independence before giving the new nation a flag. In June, 1777, Congress received a petition from the Indian Nation for one sample of the flag of the United States. Three strings of wampum accompanied the request. The Congressmen, surprised and embarrassed that the nation had no flag, immediately resolved that the United States be symbolized by thirteen stripes, alternately red and white, and thirteen white stars on a blue ground. Congress did not specify how the stars were to be arranged. The flag pictured here, with twelve stars in a circle and one in the center, was typical of the period 1777-1795. It was found in a house in Putnam County, New York.

The admission of Kentucky and Vermont to the Union in 1795 stirred a controversy over the future of the flag. Some Congressmen protested that altering the flag whenever a new state joined the union would be a flagrant waste of money. A majority of the legislators disagreed, and added two stars and two stripes to the flag. In 1818, when the Union had grown to twenty states, Congress resolved that the flag forever consist of thirteen stripes and, on the ground of blue, one white star for each state. Increasing the number of stripes, Congress reasoned, would diminish the dignity and visual power of the flag.

Rembrandt Peale. *Thomas Jefferson*, 1805. Oil on canvas. Gift of Thomas J. Bryan, 1867.306.

From his diplomatic post in Paris, Jefferson read with interest the latest reports about the movement for constitutional reform. But he felt none of the urgency that impelled his friends Washington and Madison to act. Jefferson was unshaken by Shays' Rebellion and reflected calmly that "a little rebellion now and then is a good thing." He reminded Washington that the monarchies of Europe made government in America, "with all its defects," seem "the happiest political situation" on earth.

BICENTENNIAL MINUTE

Chancellor Livingston: Judge, Diplomat and Advocate of the Constitution

by Eugene A. Gaer, Esq.

For New Yorkers, perhaps more than others, April 30, 1789, marked the conclusion of the revolutionary era in American history. On that day, George Washington was inaugurated first President under the new federal Constitution. The well-remembered event is commemorated by a statue of George Washington on the steps of Federal Hall on Wall Street—on the site of a building which in 1789 was also New York City Hall.

Many of us are familiar with the scene: the new President, already regarded as the symbol of the new nation, solemnly swearing to "preserve, protect and defend the Constitution of the United States" before a crowd of his fellow citizens. But who was it who administered the oath? There was as yet no national government, much less a Chief Justice to head the unformed federal judiciary.

Members of the New York bar may be proud to learn that the oath was administered by New York's Chancellor Robert R. Livingston, a judge and diplomat who played a significant role throughout the revolutionary and early national period, even though often overshadowed by more brilliant, if less socially prominent, contemporaries. One of Livingston's distinctions was his role in New York's ratification of the Constitution. Chancellor Livingston—the title "Chancellor" is always prefixed to his name to distinguish him from other Robert Livingstons who were also prominent in our early history—was born in 1746 into one of the most eminent families of the Province of New York. Like their close relatives, the Van Rensselaers, Beekmans and Schuylers, the Livingstons controlled vast tracts of land in the Hudson Valley and in unsettled areas west of the Hudson, and were in time not above speculating in lands seized from Tory sympathizers. Indeed, one curious aspect of New York's role in the revolution was the adherence of these great aristocrats to the cause of liberty and independence, even while steadfastly maintaining semi-feudal rights over their own tenant farmers.

When the aristocratic families held together, they were usually able to dominate New York politics. When they splintered, the reverberations were felt throughout the political system. Thus, the party system in the Province, and later the State, of New York owed less to differences between social classes than to differences within an aristocracy where each family often had multiple interests in land, commerce, finance and the law.

Livingston graduated from King's College (now Columbia University), where he distinguished himself as a student exponent of American "liberty." After an unstructured apprenticeship, he was admitted to the bar in 1768 and for a few years practiced in partnership with his later rival John Jay, the future Governor and first Chief Justice of the United States.

Denied a chance

In 1775, Livingston was sent to Philadelphia as one of New York's delegates to the Continental Congress. Chosen in June 1776 to serve with Jefferson, Adams and Franklin on the five-person committee charged with drafting the Declaration of Independence, Livingston was denied by a chain of circumstances the opportunity either to vote for the Declaration or to sign it.

During the central part of the revolution, Livingston was at least as active in local New York politics as in national politics. In early 1777, he was a member of the Kingston convention which adopted the first constitution of the independent State of New York. Livingston was active in drafting that constitution, and as a consequence he was chosen Chancellor of the new state.

The position of Chancellor was an unusual one under the state's legal system. In colonial times the governor had usually served as chancellor ex officio, dispensing equity himself. The Chancellor of the new state sat in a separate Chancery Court which inherited the royal Governor's equity jurisdiction, and was essentially an equal to the Chief Justice of the State Supreme Court. Besides judging cases, he served along with the Governor, Chief Justice and other Supreme Court justices on the "Council of Revision" which had the power to veto laws passed by the Legislature.

Livingston was to hold the office of Chancellor for 24 years, during much of which time he combined it with other significant public office. (Holding multiple offices was common in that period; his younger brother Edward was to be simultaneously the United States Attorney of the District of New York and the Mayor of New York City at the start of a long career which was capped by service as Andrew Jackson's Secretary of State.) From the fragmentary surviving records, it appears that the Chancellor held court sporadically wherever he happened to be—in New York City, Albany or at Clermont, his estate in what is now Columbia County. Almost no reported decisions or rulebooks have survived from Livingston's Chancery Court, particularly from the period before 1785.

Sidetracked by war

In the late 1770s, sitting as Chancellor was not Livingston's most important task—helping to win the revolution was. Without resigning his judicial post, Livingston returned to the Continental Congress and in 1781 was elected the first Secretary of Foreign Affairs under the Articles of Confederation. Before that time, foreign affairs had been managed by a committee of the Congress itself. Consolidating power in the hands of one secretary should have provided greater unity and coherence to foreign policy. However, as at other stages in his career, Livingston was overshadowed by his collaborators and nominal subordinates: Franklin in France, Jay in Spain and Adams in the Netherlands. Thus Livingston exercised only limited diplomatic powers. Once independence was achieved, Livingston recognized that his two offices could not easily be reconciled; he therefore resigned the foreign affairs post.

The mid-1780s are a controversial period in American history. For some historians, they represent the "critical period" in our history, when petty bickering within and among the states almost caused the enterprise of independence to founder. For others, the Articles of Confederation represent a lost opportunity for America to have developed very differently as a far more decentralized and (perhaps) democratic society than it became.

Historians have debated too over what political and social forces may have been responsible for the new Constitution of 1787. Some would see it as primarily directed at alleviating American weakness in international relations, but the extensive attention given to domestic issues indicates that the framers must have had broader goals. Others stress that it was a conservative document designed to dampen revolutionary excesses, but find it difficult to explain why many prominent opponents of ratification were land owners. One well-known theory attempts to reconcile these contradictions by stressing that the Constitution appealed especially to speculators in currency and bonds issued by the states, who wanted a strong national government capable of insuring payment of these issues. As this fiscal policy would arguably harm the landed interests, many of them became Anti-Federalists.

These theories offer little clue to why Livingston should have supported ratification. As a state court judge, he must have been unenthusiastic about the establishment of a competing federal judiciary. As one of the leading land owners of New York (who had little investment in paper property), he had nothing to gain from the fiscal policies associated with the Federalists. Indeed, in later years Livingston was aligned with the party of Jefferson and George Clinton, which absorbed the bulk of the Anti-Federalists of the ratification period.

Nonetheless in the crucial New York debate over ratification, Livingston joined with his rivals Hamilton and Jay to support the Constitution. Certainly one special perspective he had was as former head of the American foreign service, where he felt keenly embarrassed by the continuing lack of power of the new nation in foreign policy: only the adoption of a strong federal government could require Great Britain, France and other European powers to accord the United States respect as a sovereign, if not equal, power on the international scene.

Livingston expressed his feelings in a July 4 address to the Society of Cincinnati (an organization of Revolutionary War veterans) while the Constitutional Convention was already meeting in Philadelphia. He condemned contemporary states for giving insufficient offices to those with "abilities & education," as well as the "leisure to attend to the affairs of government." With respect to foreign policy, he asked:

"Who but owns that we are at this moment colonies for every purpose but that of internal taxation of the nation from whom we vainly hoped our swords had freed us?"

In the ratification convention which met in Poughkeepsie in June 1788, Livingston represented Federalist New York County rather than Columbia, where a Livingston family split permitted an Anti-Federalist landslide. His pro-ratification views were in a distinct minority of the delegates when they convened, but as Chancellor, he was entitled to give the keynote speech. Livingston is credited with the parliamentary strategy of having the entire Constitution considered as a single document before any vote would be taken on any individual portions. It is thought that if individual portions had been voted on separately, the Constitution might have been defeated before pressure could build up for ratification. However, because the opponents had their own reasons for delay, Livingston's proposal was adopted.

At the Convention, Livingston, working closely with Hamilton and Jay, was most successful in negotiating behind the scenes with wavering delegates. It is doubtful that Livingston's speeches to the convention, which were generally marked by a haughty, aristocratic tone, could have been very effective in bringing over avowedly Anti-Federalist delegates elected by ordinary farmers and workers.

Livingston's most distinguished biographer, George Dangerfield, theorizes that New York's ultimate vote for ratification resulted neither from debates nor backroom negotiation, but from the realization (once word arrived that New Hampshire and Virginia had voted for ratification) that New York would be desperately isolated if it failed to go along. In addition there was widespread fear that the southern counties (i.e., Long Island, Westchester and the present New York City), would form their own state to avoid being shut out from the commerce of the ratifying states. Thus, the New York Convention, faced with the inevitable, ratified the Constitution by a vote of 30 to 27 (with other "yes" votes probably in reserve). As one of the three leaders of the ratification cause at Poughkeepsie, Livingston is entitled to a generous measure of credit for this result.

In future years, Livingston was to add to his record of achievements. Perhaps the most important was his work as Jefferson's minister to France, when he seized the opportunity to purchase Louisiana. But of all events in his life, perhaps none deserves to be as well remembered in this Bicentennial year, as the brief moment on April 30, 1789, when Livingston stood on the balcony of New York City Hall at the focal point of all eyes in America and proclaimed: "It is done. Long live George Washington, President of the United States."

Naval Parade in New York City, April 29, 1899, Centennial Celebration of Washington's Inauguration, Photograph by Richard Hoe Lawrence. Collection of The New-York Historical Society.

New Yorkers embarked on a grand three-day commemoration of the inauguration of George Washington and the launching of the new federal government in 1789. The festivities began with a naval parade down the East River, around the Battery and onward to Governors Island. President Harrison, cabinet officials and other dignitaries sailed on the steamer Erastus Wiman, surrounded by a throng of naval vessels. A crew of shipmasters from the Marine Society of the Port of New York rowed the President ashore. Members of the same society had rowed President Washington from Elizabethport to the foot of Wall Street one hundred years earlier.

Industrial Parade in New York City, May 1, 1889, Centennial Celebration of Washington's Inauguration, Photograph by Richard Hoe Lawrence. Collection of The New-York Historical Society.

Thousands of New Yorkers participated in a huge civilian parade to celebrate the one hundredth anniversary of George Washington's inauguration and the *launching of the new federal government. The marchers assembled at 57th Street and proceeded down Fifth Avenue to Broadway, and along Broadway to Canal Street. Triumphal stone arches were erected across Fifth Avenue "to give further brilliance to the great occasion," read the Program of Parades. The arches at 23rd Street and 26th Street were demolished, but the Washington Square arch still stands.*

Rembrandt Peale. *George Washington*, 1835. Oil on canvas. Bequest of Caroline Phelps Stokes. 1910.3.

On May 25th, the delegates began the great debate by unanimously electing George Washington to be President of the Convention. His presence lent enormous prestige and legitimacy to the Convention's work.

BICENTENNIAL
MINUTE

The Bill of Rights: Desirable, Redundant, or Dangerous?

by Prof. Earl Phillips, Esq.

The first 10 amendments of the federal Constitution, the Bill of Rights, are redundant in a certain sense. They are redundant in the sense that they are all implied in the fact that the federal government has no authority except that delegated to it by the people and the states through the Constitution. None of the powers given to the President, the Congress or the Supreme Court can be stretched to include, for example, the authority to single out one religion for a preferred position vis-a-vis other religions, as the English had singled out the Anglican Church. Nor could any of the delegated powers be construed as including the authority to prohibit the keeping and bearing of arms. Hence, the Establishment Clause and the Second Amendment are, in the strictest sense, unnecessary.

Still, the Anti-Federalists, chief among them Patrick Henry of Virginia, feared the central government which the Constitution would create. They feared that it would, in time, become another George III, taxing them as he had, diluting their rights of property as he had and invading the areas rightly subject only to the sovereignty of the several states. They believed that the central government, too, would tyrannize by sending "swarms of officers, to harass our people, and eat out our substance."

Articles preferred

Having thrown off one oppressive government, Patrick Henry and his fellows hoped to prevent the creation of a new one. Henry and the other Anti-Federalists preferred the Articles of Confederation to the Constitution proposed by James Madison, also of Virginia, and Alexander Hamilton of New York. The Anti-Federalists understood as well as Madison and Hamilton that a government of delegated powers was a government with limited powers. They understood, for instance, that the federal government could place no prior restraint on the press because no power delegated to the federal government contained any authority to abrogate the press' freedom in that way. But the proposed Constitution did not say so! It did not say so! The powers granted by the Constitution were expressed; but the limits on the federal government were merely implied. One could easily ignore the limits were one bent on expanding the powers.

And the Anti-Federalists believed that this is precisely what would have happened. They believed that the Constitution would eventually be construed as granting to the central government a vast variety of unspecified powers, lurking under the generality of its phraseology, which would prove highly dangerous to the liberties of the people and the rights of the states. Therefore, they argued, if there has to be a Constitution to replace the Articles of Confederation, let it at least expressly state some of the limits on the authority of the central government. Let it also expressly state the limit on delegated power: the fact that the power of the central government is limited to those powers delegated to it and encompasses no others.

Bill of Rights opposed

Madison and Hamilton did not want a Bill of Rights. They thought it dangerous. They feared that, if the limits on the power of the central government were specified, it would soon come to be thought that those were the only limits on federal power. However, they eventually promised a Bill of Rights when they perceived that one was necessary to achieve ratification of the Constitution. The Constitutional Convention adopted the proposed Constitution, without a Bill of Rights, on September 17, 1787. On June 21, 1788, nine states had ratified the Constitution. Then Virginia ratified, on June 25, 1788. New York followed the next day, on June 26, 1788, but with a recommendation that a Bill of Rights be approved. In due course, a Bill of Rights consisting of 12 amendments to the Constitution was proposed. Of these, 10 were ratified by the requisite number of states and went into effect on September 15, 1791.

The first eight amendments set out some of the inherent limits on the authority of the central government with only delegated powers. These range from the inability of Congress to make a law respecting an establishment of religion, through the prohibition on cruel and unusual punishments. The Tenth Amendment spells out the general principle that delegated power is limited power. It makes this clear by stating, "The powers not delegated to the United States by the Constitution, nor prohibited by it to the States, are reserved to the United States respectively, or to the people." This neither adds to the powers delegated to the central government nor subtracts from them. It simply makes clear that, since the central government enjoys only those powers delegated to it, the people, acting through their state governments, remained free to legislate or not as they would on all other matters.

The Ninth Amendment was designed to forestall the dangers that Madison and Hamilton saw in the specification in the first eight amendments of certain limits on the power of the central government. The Federalists feared that the Bill of Rights would be construed as containing the only limits on the federal government. Such a construction would expand the powers of the federal government far beyond the powers delegated to it and, indeed, could produce a new George III, or a Congress comparable to Cromwell's Parliament, or even a judicial dictatorship. Consequently, the Federalists wanted the Bill of Rights to make clear that the first eight amendments did not contain all the limits on federal power. They wanted it clearly understood that the primary limit on federal power was the fact that the central government had no powers except the relatively few delegated to it in the body of the Constitution. Hence, they saw to it that the Bill of Rights also stated that "The enumeration in the Constitution of certain rights shall not be construed to deny or disparage others retained by the people." In the event, were the fears of Anti-Federalist and Federalist justified? Did the measures they took to avoid the dangers they foresaw prove effective? Perhaps, but there is no doubt of the commitment of both factions to limited central government, nor of the magnificence of their combined attempt to preserve our liberties.

Ashen B. Durand. *James Madison,* 1835. Oil on canvas. Gift of the New York Gallery of Fine Arts, 1858.10.

James Madison campaigned tirelessly for a Constitutional Convention. "What may be the result of this political experiment cannot be foreseen," he confessed to Jefferson. But the "mortal diseases" of the existing Confederation and "the unwise and wicked" state laws imperiling property and personal liberties necessitated a change in government. For many months, Madison read the histories of ancient and modern republics and labored over a complete plan of national government. By presenting his Virginia Plan on the opening day, Madison seized the opportunity to guide the Convention away from a mere revision of the Articles of Confederation. He was determined to lead the union out of a weak confederation into a national system of government.

Three times within a single generation, delegates met in the Assembly Room of the Old State House in Philadelphia and broke with the past to forge new political compacts. The Declaration of Independence called a nation into existence; the Articles of Confederation replaced an informal union with a formal central government; the federal Constitution created a new instrument of government which has endured for two hundred years. From May 25 to September 17, 1787, fifty-five delegates from twelve states labored in the summer's heat to fulfill Congress' instruction to "render the federal Constitution adequate to the exigencies of government."

George Washington presided with vigor and tact over the intense and extended debate and the hard-won compromises. In the closing moments of the convention, Benjamin Franklin observed the sun with extended rays carved on the president's chair and predicted a happy future for the new republic: "I have ... often in the course of the Session ... looked [at the sun] without being able to tell whether it was rising or setting: But now at length I have the happiness to know that it is a rising and not a setting Sun."

**BICENTENNIAL
MINUTE**

The History and Content of New York's Constitution: An Incomplete Primer

by Daniel Turbow, Esq.

As the populace of the United States dedicates substantial attention to that Constitution which governs it as a whole, it is only fitting that the people of the State of New York pause to consider their own fundamental law. The New York Constitution is a direct descendant of a document which is older than the federal Constitution—indeed, older than the Articles of Confederation. New York's Constitution is also substantially longer than its national counterpart, setting forth edicts upon subjects which impact upon every citizen of this State, as well as those which by their terms concern only the residents of the village of Saranac Lake. Notwithstanding its import, however, otherwise knowledgeable lawyers and laypersons know little of either the history or content of the State charter. While we cannot hope here to fill this void completely, we shall attempt to convey a taste of some of those matters, both the majestic and the not-so-majestic, which invest that document's past and substance.

Adopted in 1777

The Constitution of New York was originally adopted on April 20, 1777. It was promulgated by the Fourth Provincial Congress, the last of such bodies elected by the people of the Colony of New York in the turbulent 13-month period following the dissolution, in April 1775, of the General Assembly— a legislature whose responsiveness to the revolutionary fervor of certain elements of its constituency was constrained by the veto power of both the Colonial Governor and the King.

The Fourth Provincial Congress was composed of many men whose names have been memorialized, if not by history, then by geographic landmark. Among its 107 members were General Nathaniel Woodhull (its President), John Jay, Robert R. Livingston, Gouverneur Morris, John Van Cortlandt and Cornelius Van Wyck. It had originally been elected in June 1776, for the express purpose of con-

sidering a resolution by the Continental Congress that a new government be established in each colony "as shall … best conduce to the happiness and safety of their constituents in particular, and America in general." By the time the Provincial Congress convened, however, an intervening event had added substantial urgency to its task. On July 9, 1776, as it gathered for the first time, it was met with a letter from the Continental Congress transmitting for its consideration the Declaration of Independence. On the same day the Provincial Congress received that historic document, with speed completely alien to modern deliberative bodies, its members resolved, "at all risk of [their] lives and fortunes," that it be approved. On the next day, the assembly voted to change its name from "The Provincial Congress of the Colony of New York," to "The Convention of the Representatives of the State of New York."

Convention of Representatives

With the adoption of the Declaration of Independence, the newly-named Convention of Representatives assumed not only the responsibility of drafting a constitution, but also the duty of governing the State. The exigencies of the Revolution made it difficult to attend immediately to either task. Nonetheless, the Convention found time on July 16, 1776, before adjourning for a two-week period to permit its members to give "unremitted attention" to "the present dangerous situation of this state," to pass several resolutions aimed at meeting the needs of the jurisdiction in that time of crisis. One created the capital offense of treason, defining the crime as, among other things, "adherent[ce] to the King of Great Britain or to her enemies of the … state." Another authorized judicial officers to continue in their duties, "providing that all processes and other … proceedings be under the authority and in the name of the State of New York." Finally, when the Convention reconvened on August 1, 1776, it appointed a committee of 13 members, including Messrs. Jay, Morris, and Livingston, to prepare and report upon a plan for a new State government.

While the framers of the federal Constitution went about their business in the relative tranquility of post-Revolution Philadelphia, the authors of New York's Constitution, meeting during the war, were not afforded a similar luxury. Together with the Convention, the drafting committee was required to change its place of business several times to avoid capture by the British. Thus, it first met in White Plains, instead of New York City, because of the imminence of British attack, and subsequently moved to several other locations including Harlem, Fishkill, Poughkeepsie and, finally, Kingston. In addition, the more pressing business of armed struggle made it difficult for some committee members to devote undivided attention to their drafting duties. For example, John Jay was required to spend substantial time fulfilling his responsibilities as a member of the committee appointed "to devise and carry into execution such measures as to them shall appear most effectual for obstructing the channel of Hudson's river or annoying the enemy's ships in their navigation of the said river." Because of similar delays, it was not until March 12, 1777, that a draft of the State Constitution, apparently prepared primarily by Jay, was presented to the Convention. The draft was debated and modified by the Convention and, on April 20, adopted as the State's first Constitution.

Despite a lengthy preamble which recites the various resolutions and events upon which the Convention based its authority (including the entire Declaration of Independence—with signatures), the first Constitution itself is not unduly prolix. Although it contains 42 Articles, most are not longer than a paragraph. It includes some provisions which reflected the unique times in which it was drafted, such as one designed to defuse potential hostility of native Indians by voiding recent fraudulent land sales contracts to which they were parties. As a whole, however, its content displays a relatively terse and insightful effort to provide substance to many of the same basic principles of political theory which motivated the rebellion against England and which were subsequently incorporated into our national charter.

Fundamental premise

Thus, its very first Article articulated the fundamental democratic premise that "no authority shall, on any pretense whatever, be exercised over the people or members of this state, but such shall be derived from and granted by them." The Constitution went on to create the machinery of a tri-partite form of government, which remains intact to this day, composed of ... a legislature, comprised of an Assembly and Senate; an executive branch, headed by the governor; and a judiciary. Most interestingly, the document also expressly set forth many of the guarantees we now commonly associate with the federal Constitution's Bill of Rights.

Inviolate rights

Thus, it provided that in trials of crimes or misdemeanors the accused "shall be allowed counsel, as in civil actions." It made "inviolate" the right to trial by jury in all cases in which such trials had been allowed in the Colony of New York. And, it expressed a form of Due Process Clause, adopted from the Magna Charta, providing that "no member of this state shall be disenfranchised, or deprived of any rights or privileges secured to the subjects of this state by this Constitution, unless by law of the land, or the judgment of his peers."

The first Constitution also secured the right to religious freedom in several ways. It prohibited "ministers of the gospel" from holding any civil or military office. In addition, in a vitally significant provision which addressed more than the topic of religion, it called for the preservation of the common law of England and the Colony of New York, except those parts "as may be construed to establish or maintain any particular denomination of Christians or their ministers, or concern the allegiance heretofore yielded to, and the supremacy, sovereignty ... claimed or exercised by, the King of Great Britain and his predecessors ... ." Finally, "to guard against that spiritual oppression and intolerance wherewith the bigotry and ambition of weak and wicked priests

and princes have scourged mankind," it declared "That the free exercise and enjoyment of religious profession and worship, without discrimination or preference, shall forever hereafter be allowed within the state to all mankind: Provided, That the liberty of conscience hereby granted shall not be so construed as to excuse acts of licentiousness, or justify practices inconsistent with the peace or safety of this state."

Radical departure

This last, "free exercise" provision, was a radical departure from the prior law of the Colony, where religious freedom was guaranteed, except to "Papists." And, while we now take for granted its protections, which remain virtually unchanged in our present State Constitution, no less a personage than John Jay, fearing foreign influences, proposed an amendment that it should not apply "to professors of the religion of the Church of Rome, who ought not to hold lands in or be admitted to, a participation of the civil rights ... " unless and until they swore in court "that no pope, priest or foreign authority on earth, hath power to absolve the subjects of this State from their allegiance to the same." Fortunately, Jay's proposal was defeated, and the tamer proviso quoted above adopted in its stead.

Not perfect

The first Constitution was not a perfect document. For example, the right to vote was generally limited to males who possessed a freehold of 20 pounds in the county of their residence, "or have rented a tenement therein of the yearly value of forty shillings ... and actually paid taxes to this state." (Commercial wealth apparently proving a significant source of political influence even then, an exception to this requirement was provided to freemen residing in the cities of Albany and New York). It also contained many provisions which did not stand the test of time, such as one creating a Council of Revision, comprised of the governor, the chancellor and judges of

the supreme court, whose duty it was to consider the constitutionality of proposed legislative acts. In addition, certain of its provisions, such as those dealing with naturalization, were mooted by history.

Nor were the framers perfect men. John Jay's proposed addendum to the free exercise provision is evidence of human shortcomings, as is the debate over a provision calling upon the legislature to abolish slavery at the conclusion of the War of Independence, which was not adopted. Nonetheless, on the whole, they produced a document which can truly be called a "constitution," in the sense that it announced the State's fundamental law, creating the machinery of government and setting the outermost boundaries of that government's power. The Constitution of today can be said to fulfill those functions, but it does much more as well. As Judge Kaye of the Court of Appeals tactfully commented in a recent address, "Given its laborious detail, our [present] Constitution may not in every phrase ring with the majesty of Chief Justice Marshall's declaration: 'It is a *constitution* we are expounding.'" (Forty-first Benjamin N. Cardozo Lecture to the Association of the Bar of the City of New York by Judge Kaye, *Dual Constitution in Practice and Principle* (Feb. 26, 1987) (reprinted in Vol. 42, No. 3 Record of the Association of the Bar) (quoting *McCulloch v. Maryland,* 4 Wheat (17 U.S.) 315, 407 (1819) *(emphasis by the Court).*

Other versions

The present State Constitution, while a direct descendant of that of 1777, is not the first of the initial Constitution's offspring. New Constitutions were adopted in 1821, 1846, and 1894. The 1894 Constitution was substantially reorganized and modified in 1938, and as subsequently amended from time to time, still governs us today. As each of these revisions built upon its predecessors, the fundamental document of 1777 grew progressively bulkier and more detailed.

Today's Constitution is comprised of only 20 Articles, compared with the 42 of its original ancestor.

However, those Articles contain a total of approximately 200 separate sections, most of which are composed of several paragraphs. While many of these provisions reflect certain of the same basic concerns as were addressed in the first Constitution, others appear to stray somewhat from the document's initial purpose.

For example, as did the first Constitution, today's Constitution scrupulously protects individual liberties. Indeed, the first Article of the present Constitution contains a Bill of Rights of 15 sections. This Article provides many of the same—or even firmer—bulwarks against the abuse of government power included in the federal Constitution.

Freedom of speech

In addition to restating the substance of the guarantees of personal liberty set forth in the first State Constitution which were discussed above, Article I also contains provisions dealing with, among other things, freedom of speech and press, self-incrimination, equal protection, unreasonable searches and seizures, habeas corpus, double jeopardy, just compensation, etc. Moreover, it contains provisions which, while not contemplated by the federal Constitution, can fairly be said to be reflective of society's evolving views of what rights require constitutional protection. For example, in 1913, following the holding of the Court of Appeals in *Ives v. South Buffalo Ry. Co.* 201 N.Y. 271 (1911), which struck down a worker's compensation law as violative of the due process clause, what is now section 18 was added to Article I, authorizing such a statutory scheme. Similarly, the Bill of Rights also guarantees the right to collective bargaining and the 40-hour work week.

Article I also contains provisions which one would not ordinarily associate with a constitution, let alone with a bill of rights. For example, its very first section restates the classic language of the first Constitution, derived from the Magna Charta, which prohibits a citizen's disenfranchisement or deprivation of rights "unless by the law of the land, or the judg-ment of his peers." But, the section goes on to demean this eloquent statement of one of our most basic principles of democracy by stating immediately thereafter, "except that the legislature may provide that there shall be no primary election held to nominate candidates for public office" under certain circumstances. One cannot help but wonder whether the parties responsible for this 1959 proviso to a doctrine held in reverence since 1215 gave sufficient consideration to whether their concerns about primary elections could not have been addressed in some other manner.

Other anomalies

Article I contains other similar anomalies. For example, section 9, which prohibits the abridgment of "the rights of the people peaceably to assemble and to petition the government," goes on to provide a detailed statement of the circumstances under which gambling will be prohibited or allowed. The careful constitutional scholar reading the section will be rewarded with learning that religious, charitable, or other similar non-profit organizations can conduct "games of chance commonly known as … bingo or lotto," if appropriate legislative authority is provided and no single prize of more than $250 is awarded.

Such meshing of the constitutionally sublime and ridiculous is not confined to Article I. Article XIV, for instance, dealing with conservation, requires the state forest preserve to "be forever kept as wild forest lands." Nonetheless, the state may give 10 acres of such land to the village of Saranac Lake for refuse disposal in return for a particular 30 acres owned by the village "on Roaring Brook, in the northern half of Lot 113, Township 11, Richards Survey."

Detailed provisions

Similar examples of such detailed provisions are found throughout the Constitution's text. Interestingly, they appear most prevalent when the document is addressing subjects which are most distant from those ordinarily associated with a consti-tution's basic purpose. For example, Article XI deals with education, the responsibility for which is today accepted as a fundamental duty of the government. In three short paragraphs, that Article, among other things, requires the state to provide free education, establishes the Board of Regents, and prohibits public aid to parochial schools. On the other hand, as Judge Kaye has noted, Article VIII, dealing with local finances, is longer than the entire federal Constitution and, one must add, substantially more difficult to parse.

Ordinary legislation a better approach?

There are many other provisions which perhaps would be more suitable for ordinary legislation. There are 39 separate sections dealing with the judiciary. By contrast, Article III of the federal charter provided in a trio of concise paragraphs the constitutional basis for all the federal courts. Does New York's Constitution really require a separate Article dealing with canals?

In short, one sees in today's Constitution many things which the framers of the first Constitution would find surprising. In large measure, these provisions reflect frequent utilization of the mechanism for amending the instrument contained in Article XIX. While criticism that the amendment process is sometimes too easy may be appropriate, it is also true that the process permits a valuable responsiveness to the voice of the citizens of the State and requires a constant re-evaluation over time of those matters considered significant enough to be addressed in the document. In any event, when one penetrates the Constitution's text to reach its essence, one finds that the basic principles set forth in 1777 remain.

The people of New York owe a great deal to those men who, in the midst of war, created such a thoughtful and lasting body of fundamental law.

(Readers interested in learning more about the subject are referred to Lincoln's Constitutional History of New York, *which provided the source for much of this article.)*

Painted silk banner carried in the Federal Procession at New York City, July 23, 1788. Gift of Mr. James S. Haring, 1903.12. restored by Ms. Kathryn Scott, 1974.

On July 23, 1788, New York City celebrated the adoption of the U.S. Constitution with cannon fire, bell ringing, and a grand parade and outdoor banquet. More than five thousand people marched in the Federal Procession. This painted silk banner was carried by the Society of Pewterers, one of the many working men's associations that marched. Pictured on the banner are a thirteen-star flag—although only ten states had ratified— a coat-of-arms inscribed "Solid and Pure," and the interior of a pewterer's shop. The New York State convention, already meeting at Poughkeepsie, ratified the Constitution three days later.

Archibald Robertson. *Federal Hall, N.Y.C.*, 1798. Watercolor and ink on paper. Given by Sophia Minton, 1864.14.

An enthusiastic city reconstructed the war-torn building on this site in 1788-1789 to welcome the new federal government. On the afternoon of April 30, 1789, President-elect George Washington stepped through the crimson damask that draped the central window, bowed repeatedly to the multitude gathered below the balcony, and waited for the crowd to quiet. After taking the oath of office, he stepped back into the Senate chamber, and read his inaugural address to Congress in an aged, trembling voice.

Congress met in Federal Hall for only a few months after the inauguration, and then made the ungrateful decision to move temporarily to Philadelphia and permanently to the shores of the Potomac River. In 1804, the original home of the federal government became the first home of The New-York Historical Society.

Biographies

Sheldon Siporin is a sole practictioner in Brooklyn. He received his law degree from the University of California—Davis. His professional memberships include the state bar, American Judges Association, American Bar Association, Brooklyn Bar Association, New York County Lawyers Association, American Arbitration Association, and the State Bar of California.

In 1986 he was one of 14 recipients chosen to receive the President's Pro Bono Award presented by the New York State Bar Association to recognize lawyers who have volunteered to donate their time and knowledge to provide civil legal services, free of charge, to the state's disadvantaged, poor, elderly and handicapped.

Robert A. Hendrickson is a partner in the law firm of Eaton & Van Winkle and the author of the definitive two-volume biography of Alexander Hamilton, tracing the life of the man who led the battle for the Constitution at the New York ratifying convention of 1788 and conceived the Federalist Papers. Mr. Hendrickson attended the University of Bensacon, France and the Sorbonne. He received his law degree from Harvard University. A prolific writer, he has also authored *The Rise and Fall of Alexander Hamilton,* 1986 Dodd Mead & Co. (paperback), *The Cashless Society* (1972), *The Future of Money* (1970), *Changing the Status of a Trust, Interstate and International Estate Planning* and other books and articles. His "Beaumarchais as a Cross Examiner" and "Law and Lawyers in Mozart" are firmly set in the heroic late eighteenth century whose Bicentennials we celebrate with each passing current year.

Dominic R. Massaro was named to the State Court of Claims by Governor Cuomo in December, 1986. He is currently on assignment as a Justice of the Supreme Court, Bronx County, Criminal Branch, and serves as chairman of the county's Commission on the Bicentennial of the U.S. Constitution. More recently, he authored "Gouverneur Morris: The Constitutional Penman Revisited" for the *Bronx County Historical Society Journal* (Fall, 1987) and "Il Miracolo della Costituzione" for *Due Mondi Review* (September, 1987).

Jane H. Hovde is a freelance writer, author, and part-time instructor in secondary schools and colleges. She received her law degree from Columbia University as well as a master's degree in history from Columbia's graduate school. Her professional memberships in addition to the New York State Bar Association include the Institute for Research and History.

She is co-author of the teacher's guide prepared for the movie, "An Empire of Reason," which describes New York's pivotal role in the ratification of the Constitution. In the Fall of 1988 her book, a biography of Jane Addams, will be published.

Eugene A. Gaer, an attorney and historian, earned his undergraduate degree from Harvard University and a law degree from Columbia University. He has also studied in the graduate history departments of the University of Wisconsin and the University of Chicago. Prior to becoming a lawyer, he taught European and American history at Roosevelt University and other colleges. He is now Vice President and General Counsel of FOJP Service Corporation, the risk management advisor for the United Jewish Appeal — Federation of Jewish Philanthropies of New York. He is secretary of the Committee on Federal Constitution.

Ernest E. Phillips is a professor of law at Fordham University School of Law. He received both his undergraduate degree and a master of law's degree from Georgetown University. He was a member of the Law Review and is currently a member of the Advisory Committee to the Family Court, Appellate Division of state Supreme Court, First Department.

Daniel Turbow is a senior litigator in the Corporation Counsel's Office of the City of New York and an adjunct assistant professor at Brooklyn Law School. He is a *magna cum laude* graduate of Brooklyn Law School and maintains professional memberships in the: American Bar Association, Federal Bar Council, and Association of the Bar of the City of New York. His New York State Bar Association activities include service as a member of the Committee on Federal Courts in addition to the Committee on Federal Constitution.

Members of the Committee on Federal Constitution

Marion Blankopf, Esq.
  Nixon, Hargrave, Devans & Doyle
Rochester

Michael W. Brody, Esq.
  Equitable Life Assurance Society of the
    United States
New York City

George A. Davidson, Esq.
  Hughes, Hubbard & Reed
New York City

Jo Ann Ellison, Esq.
  Lord Day & Lord
New York City

Edward J. Ennis, Esq.
New York City

Eugene A. Gaer
  FOJP Service Corporation
New York City

Douglas Gross, Esq.
  Hofheimer, Gartlir, Gottlieb & Gross
New York City

Jon H. Hammer, Esq.
New York City

Robert A. Hendrickson, Esq.
  Eaton & Van Winkle
New York City

Edward Himmelfarb, Esq.
  United States Department of Justice
Washington, D.C.

Jane H. Hovde, Esq.
New York City

Judge Dominic R. Massaro
  Supreme Court
Bronx

Charles J. Moxley, Jr., Esq.
  Jones, Hirsch, Connors & Bull
New York City

Don P. Murnane, Esq.
  Haight, Gardner, Poor & Havens
New York City

Charles M. Newman, Esq.
New York City

Robert S. Peck, Esq.
  American Bar Association
Washington, D.C.

Prof. Ernest E. Phillips, Esq.
  Fordham Law School
New York City

Sheldon Siporin, Esq.
Brooklyn

William M. Thomas, Jr., Esq.
  Hughes, Hubbard & Reed
New York City

Daniel Turbow, Esq.
  Corporation Counsel's Office
New York City

Judge Penny M. Wolfgang
  Supreme Court
Buffalo

CHAIR
Nicole A. Gordon, Esq.
  New York State Commission on Government
    Integrity
New York City

In a 1788 celebration of the impending ratification of the Constitution, New Yorkers honored one of the Constitution's foremost champions, Alexander Hamilton. He may be the man standing on top of the wall at the left, receiving accolades from the special horse-drawn float carrying a 27-foot replica of a frigate.